FLOYD ON FISH

FLOYD ON FISH

KEITH FLOYD

BRITISH BROADCASTING CORPORATION
in association with **ABSOLUTE PRESS**

Design and art direction/Glyn Davies

Photographs/Andrew Whittuck
Styling/Bobbie Baker
Food preparation/Jane Suthering

Chapter opening illustrations/David Sim
Technical illustrations/Will Giles and Sandra Pond

Published by the British Broadcasting Corporation
35 Marylebone High Street
London W1M 4AA
in association with Absolute Press (publishers)
14 Widcombe Crescent, Widcombe Hill, Bath, Avon

ISBN 0 563 20444 3 (Hardback)
ISBN 0 563 20422 2 (Paperback)

Typeset in Futura Light by
Rowland Phototypesetting Ltd
Bury St Edmunds, Suffolk
Printed and bound by
Mackays, Chatham, Kent
Colour printing by Jolly and Barber Ltd, Rugby

'What on earth is this?'
'A piece of cod, sir.'
'The piece of cod which passeth all understanding.'

Attributed to Sir Edwin Lutyens, to a waiter at Brooks.

CONTENTS

All these are *approximate* conversions, which have either been rounded up or down. In a few recipes it has been necessary to modify them very slightly. Never mix metric and imperial measures in one recipe; stick to one system or the other.

WEIGHTS

½ oz	10 g
1	25
1½	40
2	50
3	75
4	110
5	150
6	175
7	200
8	225
9	250
10	275
12	350
13	375
14	400
15	425
1 lb	450
1¼	550
1½	700
2	900
3	1.4 kg
4	1.8
5	2.3

VOLUME

1 fl oz	25 ml
2	50
3	75
5 (¼ pint)	150
10 (½)	275
15 (¾)	400
1 pint	570
1¼	700
1½	900
1¾	1 litre
2	1.1
2¼	1.3
2½	1.4
2¾	1.6
3	1.75
3¼	1.8
3½	2
3¾	2.1
4	2.3
5	2.8
6	3.4
7	4.0
8 (1 gal)	4.5

MEASUREMENTS

¼ inch	0.5 cm
½	1
1	2.5
2	5
3	7.5
4	10
6	15
7	18
8	20.5
9	23
11	28
12	30.5

OVEN TEMPERATURES

Mark	1	275°F	140°C
	2	300	150
	3	325	170
	4	350	180
	5	375	190
	6	400	200
	7	425	220
	8	450	230
	9	475	240

Low tide at Cancale and the beach stretches far to the Brittany horizon. The sun has resigned, washed out by the early evening grey. A niggling wind is blowing, rippling the water in the little oyster basins that clutter the beach like a system of crude sewage tanks. Concrete tanks that trap the receding tides are filled with sacks of oysters. Stumps, clustered with mussels, stand like rotten gibbets way down to the muddy sea.

A toothless woman packs her beach stall, folds the money into her apron and bounces off across the shingle in a battered *deux chevaux*. The oyster farmers, another day over, roar away in yellow oilskins on orange tractors to the comfort of a bar in the village. Crocodiles of multicoloured school children, their natural history lesson over, snake off across the flats to waiting buses. The last tourist rolls up her beach mat and makes for the hotel. Seabirds wheel and cry over a beach, derelict and deserted of human life.

Deserted that is except for a BBC film unit, which in no way can be described as human. We are about to shoot the last sequence of *Floyd on Fish*. Just one last short sequence and after nearly a year of catching, cooking, eating, talking, breathing fish, we are at an end.

The director wants a good pay off. 'You know, just one last plumptious little darling. A little sizzler to go out on.'

M. Mindeau, a charming diminutive Frenchman who has spent the day courteously guiding me around the oyster beds, waits uncomprehendingly as the director explains what he wants.

'Roll up your sleeve, pluck an oyster from the basin, hold it to camera. Do the piece again where M. Mindeau says the Portuguese oysters are the mushrooms and the flat Helford ones are the truffles. Translate it in a piece to camera and . . . .'

'I am not eating another oyster!'

'Just put your hand in the basin, grab the ****** oyster, open it and eat it.'

The director, tall and plump, starts towards me, pointing a threatening finger. I say, 'Listen, I've been eating these things since seven this morning, as well as clams and spider crabs and cockles, whelks, winkles and raw mussels. Not only today, but every day we've been filming. Fish! I loved it, now I hate it. I won't eat another oyster for you or anyone else.'

M. Mindeau looks at me, then at the director. He smiles and shrugs his shoulders. I know what he is thinking. And I feel guilty, so I swallow the oyster and smile.

The director says, 'Cut. It's a wrap.'

The cameraman looks at him. 'Keith's smile was a little forced, you know. Happy with that?'

Something in me snaps. I choke on the half ingested oyster and collapse into hysterics. M. Mindeau just smiles; a sad, pitying smile.

But fish is still my favourite dish. Honestly. And I hope that this book will help to make it yours.

As a small boy I played spaceships with the presses and machines in my grandfather's workshop. As he stumped around on his tin leg, a mouth full of nails and whistling some mournful tune, sharpening knives and cutting leather as he remade farmers' boots or cursing as he replaced a stiletto heel on a woman's shoe, I would start to think about eating. At twelve noon the brewery siren would sound, summoning the village to lunch. My mother was and still is one of the best cooks I know, but staying with my granny in those days was something special; everything tasted extra good because it was fresh. Indeed, she was often paid for the repairs that grandad had done with an enamel bowl of thick, yellow-crusted clotted cream, or a basket of freshly gathered mushrooms, or a hare or even a brace of pheasants. Eggs came from her own chickens, vegetables from the garden. Some Sundays grandad would have to kill a chicken for lunch, and I smile to this day at the absurdity of him lurching around the workshop yard, badly handicapped by the artificial leg, after a headless chicken still running for all its worth. It never occurred to me then that this was a pretty barbarous way of dispatching the Sunday lunch.

There was always a larder full of pickles and preserves, always the remains of a cold joint, or a home-cured ham to raid. But for me, as a small boy, the important things about my granny's cooking were the volume and the choice. Two main courses were always on offer for lunch, except for Monday, when it was cold meat, mashed potatoes and pickles. Some Saturday nights my grandfather would collect snails and cook them in the fire, on others maybe pig's trotters would be eaten in front of the hearth with mustard and strong, real malt vinegar. The highlight of the week for me, however, was Friday lunch. Fresh fish. Either steamed cod and parsley with boiled potatoes and carrots, or deep-fried haddock cooked in dripping with really brilliant chips. I had both. Herrings were bought to bake in vinegar for tea; and tea fish (salted and dried cod) which we would have for Sunday breakfast. It smelt like old boots, but I crave for the taste to this day.

Both my mother and grandmother were adventurous cooks, but all in all in those early years, until I was 14, I had only experienced cod, haddock, herrings, tea fish and the occasional plaice. Until one May morning when I caught my first fish.

Like kids everywhere, the fishing bug suddenly bit me. I pestered everyone to get me a rod and take me fishing. At last, using the silk thread from the cobbler's shop and a bamboo pole from the garden, my father constructed a rod. We dug lively red worms from the compost heap and set out through the village to the chestnut-tree-lined lane that led to a little reservoir, where, said my uncle, there were fish; huge fish, with teeth like bananas. We crouched by the triangular pool under some elder trees and set up the tackle. It was not quite bent-pin stuff, but very nearly.

I cast. The float had hardly settled before it shot under the water and the line went taut. I was petrified. The rod was jumping out of my hands and dad was shouting, 'Reel in, reel in.' But I couldn't. So he grabbed the rod and roughly dragged the crazily flapping fish out of the water and on to the bank. (It wasn't until many years later that he admitted to me that he knew nothing about fishing.)

The fish was dark blue on the back, but its sides dissolved into pale gold and red and orange spots, ringed with violet and emerald. Overcome with excitement I stooped to pick it up. It flapped away and I tumbled into the nettles in my haste to recover it. I plucked up the courage to knock it out, and then wrapped it in dock leaves. We caught four more before the sun flooded on to the little reservoir and blinded us with dazzling reflections. Dad said we must go home. We didn't know the names of the fish, so I raced ahead to look at the *Observer Book of Fish*.

'Hey dad They're trout! We can eat them, can't we?'

I wasn't shocked when mum filleted, battered and deep fried the trout, like cod. They tasted good, but something inside me said there was more to fish eating than deep frying.

I resolved to find out.

The opportunity came when dad said the summer holidays were too long for a boy of my age to idle away. I must get a job, which was easy enough in the Wiveliscombe of the 1950s. So I became an odd-job boy at the Lion Hotel, where I peeled potatoes, weeded the cobblestone courtyard, or watched Mrs Maxwell poach whole trout in wine and water and herbs and make yellow sauces with eggs and butter! A long way from cod and parsley sauce, indeed.

I spent my spare time in the holidays fishing. By now I had acquired the proper gear and many a morning at dawn I would cycle a dozen or more miles to new water, rumoured to be packed with specimen fish. One autumn, at a lake near Bishop's Lydeard where I hoped to catch a pike, I found that I had forgotten my all-important sandwiches. The only food I had with me was stale bread, bait with which I hoped to catch some small fish to use as live bait for the pike. It was absurd to cycle home, for I would have missed the morning's best chances. Inspiration came to me. I had caught a couple of small perch, I had lots of stale bread, and there were still blackberries and pine-nuts around. I lit a fire inside a small circle of stones and sort of grilled the perch. Then I soaked the stale bread in water, stuffed pine-nuts and blackberries into the 'dough' to make small cakes and cooked them over the hot stones. They were delicious. Those were the days!

And I didn't catch a pike. I was to have to wait more than 25 years before I finally caught one, while filming *Floyd on Fish*.

There were not many restaurants in the provinces, even in the early sixties. My first visit to a real restaurant, at the age of 17, was a truly memorable one. I was taken to the Hole in the Wall, Bath, by my boss at the time, the editor of the *Bristol Evening Post*. I was overwhelmed. And after a meal of thick fish soup and salmon baked in pastry (something of a cliché these days, but then George Perry-Smith was without peer), followed by chocolate St Emilion, I was ruined for life. I became a gastronaut.

Happily, my career on the paper did not work out, and for some extraordinary reason I joined the army and became a second lieutenant in the Tank Regiment. The food in the mess was dreadful – although the best kippers I have ever eaten were at Catterick. My brother officers had no interest in it, and I, with little to do, became the messing member. So, I bought some Elizabeth David books and set to work on our cook, a certain Corporal Feast! Soon, instead of brown soup and roast chicken, followed by devils on horseback, we were eating fish soups and hare terrines à la Mrs David. I am sad to say that no-one commented on the change of menus and style. But I owe a debt to Corporal Feast. He was willing to accept my ideas, or should I say my interpretation of Elizabeth David's ideas, and in exchange he taught me the essential basic skills, such as how to chop an onion, make a roux, or bone a chicken.

Of course, as a young subaltern, the living was easy and quite unrealistic. On leaving the luxury of the mess after my three-year stint, I found myself unemployed and unemployable, standing bewildered and alone on civvy street. A street filled with people in kaftans and sandals. Even architects were wearing flowered ties. The head chef at the Royal Hotel, Bristol, was a mountain of a man; over six feet and beetroot faced, like Mervyn Peake's Swelter. He stared down the swollen promontory of his nose in utter disbelief at my request.

'You? You want to be a cook. What does an officer want to be a cook for?'

'I'd be happy peeling potatoes, even.'

'You haven't deserted, have you?'

Outside his little glass cubicle in the centre of the kitchen, dozens of chefs and apprentices scurried around the black slabs of stoves, stirring, slicing, chopping, straining, or sniffing into huge cauldrons.

'I'll do anything as long as it's in the kitchen,' I pleaded.

'I'll tell you what. If you can answer one simple question, I'll give you a go. What,' he said, with a glimmer of a smile, 'is the difference between a waiter and a bucket of pig swill?'

I took a deep breath.

'The bucket?'

He opened the office door and called to a boy many years younger than I. 'This is *Mister* Floyd. Show him the potato peeler.'

I spent my first hot day in a kitchen, peeling potatoes in a subterranean gloom, dressed in Chelsea boots and an immaculate three-piece suit. No-one spoke to me.

I went the rounds of hotels and restaurants for nearly two years before I took the insane step of opening my own restaurant. Of course, I had no idea how to run a business, never mind a restaurant. On opening night, I cooked desperately in four inches of wine and débris that sloshed about the kitchen floor. The more tolerant guests accepted my apologies and drank me dry for free, the others just walked out. At three that morning, cut, burnt, bruised and drunk, I wept. My God, what had I done? By the end of the first week I was gaining control; things weren't so bad. Within three months they queued for the doors to open. I seldom saw light of day. As fast as the till filled up, the faster the bank balance diminished. With hindsight, I would have enjoyed the Foreign Legion more or taken monastic vows with a lighter heart.

However, all that was nearly 20 years ago, and it would require a whole book to tell the tales of the 11 or so restaurants I have owned or run, in France, Spain and England during that time. It is a book that I will write. If ever I finish this one, that is. It has come as something of a shock to discover that writing is just as hard as running a restaurant. Especially if you are sitting in comfort in a remote and elegant house on the edge of a cliff, overlooking the huge beauty of Porthcurno Cove, virtually at Land's End, with a bottle of wine by your side and a glass in your hand.

Excuse me now. I must leave the typewriter and return to the kitchen to clean the mussels for lunch. As J. P. Donleavy said: 'Life is just a bowl of cherries – as long as you get most of them.'

PS   Despite a massive campaign by the Sea Fish Industry Authority, sales of fresh and frozen fish have declined in Britain. As a nation we eat about 2 lb of fish *per household* a year. By my estimation that's about one and a half unidentified frying objects per person per week. Strange that we eat so little when the fishermen of this country land so much, and in such variety.

I'm not surprised that sales of fresh fish have declined – it's very difficult to buy it. Fish shops – the traditional kind with marble slabs simply shimmering with whiting, herring, salmon, prawns, dog fish, John Dory, halibut, hake, trout, shark, mussels, whelks and winkles – have become a thing of the past. Instead, carton manufacturers dictate what we shall eat with their appealing/appalling oblong boxes piled high in the frosted cabinets of supermarkets (although Waitrose now makes an effort with fresh fish). But it's more than that. We have become frightened of fish – we've lost the nerve of our grandmothers.

It's our fault. For accepting frozen dover soles and breaded scampi in restaurants. It's *our* fault for buying scampi flavoured crisps. It's *our* fault for not encouraging the fishmongers. The trouble is we are lazy snobs. Much better, we often say, a frozen salmon or some other exotic and expensive fish than a simple plate of fresh sprats or dog fish; because we'd rather be talking about it, glass in hand in our sitting room that has been designed by the marketing man, than rolling up our sleeves around the kitchen table where real life, love, food, and fun belong.

South Minack, May 1985

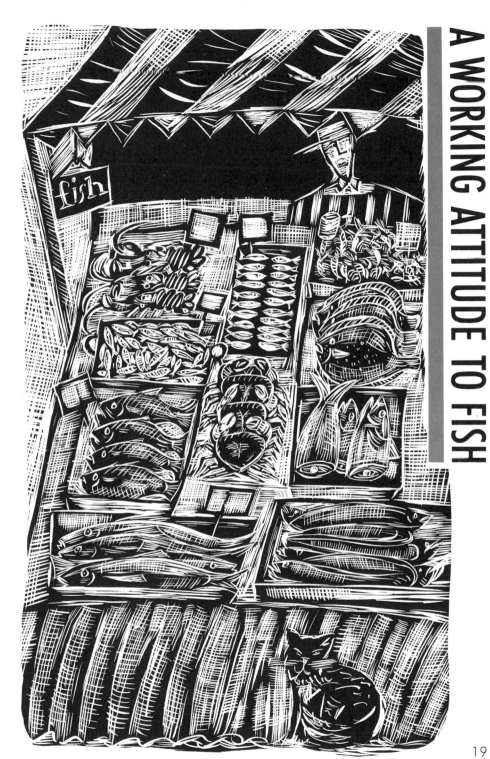

fish

For the optimistic cook, fish is a dazzling challenge – over 50 varieties are available in Britain and there are countless ways of preparing them. In this book I have chosen a few of my favourite dishes, but you must not stop there. You could cook fish every day of the year and not repeat a single dish. But like all worthwhile pastimes – and cooking should be looked upon as a hobby, not a chore – there are essential disciplines and rules, and the most important of these is to ignore the unidentified frozen objects in the freezer cabinets of stores and to make friends with your fishmonger. And buy only the *freshest* of fish.

CHOOSING FISH

Fish from the sea should smell of seawater, not of fish. The eyes should be bright, almost alert, and the gills bright red. Don't be afraid to prod and poke the fish before you buy it – it should be firm and tight, not soggy or flaky. Never buy pre-cooked shellfish, especially lobster or crayfish (crawfish). They must be alive and kicking. They should also feel heavy and dense.

It is wise to plan a fish meal in advance. Order your fish and then choose the recipe. This method will ensure that you will not have to compromise the dish by discovering at the last moment that you missed a vital ingredient or that the fish was unavailable. People plan visits to the theatre and trips to the country well in advance, they dress up for the occasion and spend time and money to ensure a good time. You must take the same attitude to your fish cookery.

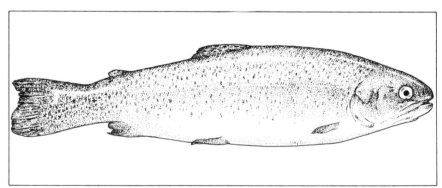

▲   Make sure the eyes are bright, and the fish feels firm

CLEANING FISH

Your fishmonger will clean the fish for you, but you should at least know the essentials:

1   Cut off all the fins.
2   Scale the fish by running a blunt knife from the tail to the head.

3 Slit open the belly and remove the intestines. Some fish (trout, for example) have a blood sac running along the backbone, so scrape this out with the point of a knife.
4 Rinse well under cold water and thoroughly dry.
(I like to leave the head on, but this is a matter of preference.)

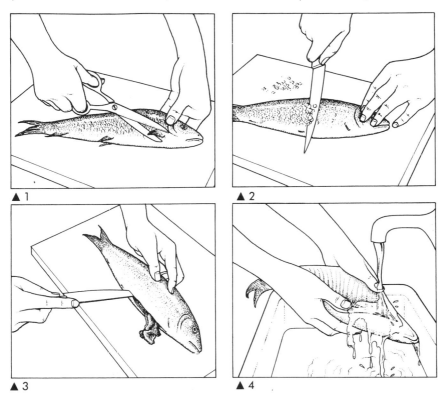

▲ 1

▲ 2

▲ 3

▲ 4

FILLETING FISH

To fillet round fish (herrings, for example):

1 Slit the belly of the cleaned fish from head to tail.
2 Squeeze your forefinger and thumb tightly around the backbone, directly behind the head, and, keeping close to the bone, draw your fingers firmly to the tail.

To fillet large round fish (cod, for example):

1 Make a vertical incision behind the head until you reach the bone.
2 Turn the knife on its side and run it along the bone to the tail.

To fillet flat fish (sole, for example):

1 Run a sharp knife along the central line of one side.

2 Lay the knife sideways, tight to the bone, and slice to the edge and the tail, at the same time lifting the fillet free with the other hand.

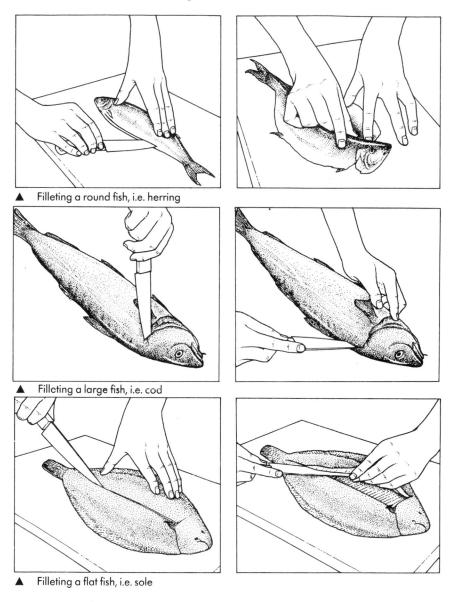

▲ Filleting a round fish, i.e. herring

▲ Filleting a large fish, i.e. cod

▲ Filleting a flat fish, i.e. sole

SKINNING FISH

1 Make an incision under the skin. **2** Prise it off with your fingers and a knife. Do not rip the flesh. You can always peel off the skin after the fish has been cooked if you find that you can't manage it before.

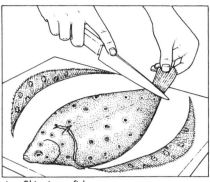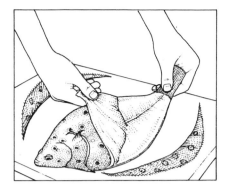

▲ Skinning a fish

METHODS OF COOKING

Most fish is either poached, fried, grilled or steamed. It is never boiled.

Poaching   This, in effect, means simmering a fish in a stock or court bouillon that does not boil. Even shellfish, such as lobster and crab, are only brought to the boil and then allowed to cook in hot water.

Frying   Small, whole fish, such as trout or perch, are best shallow fried in butter. Deep frying is only suitable for battered fish.

Steaming   The fish is laid on a buttered and covered dish and then placed over a simmering pan of water, a method much favoured by oriental cooks. Another version requires the pan, over which the fish is placed, to have perforations to allow steam through to cook directly.

Grilling   The golden rule for grilling is: always turn on the grill well in advance of the cooking time. The outer skin of the fish should be sealed quickly, thus allowing the flesh to cook from the inside.

Barbecueing   Apart from the freshness of the fish, the important point about barbecueing is the technique itself.

Ideally I would encourage you to build a sympathetic stone barbecue on the terrace but no doubt either the skills of the advertising industry or the lack of space will have resulted in a visit to your nearest garden centre. Your barbecue must be robust and substantial and capable of giving out sustained and intense heat. As well as the barbecue itself, you will need a fish-shaped grip for fish and a couple of sandwich grips able to take 10 sardines at a time.

If you can add some aromatic wood, such as vine twigs, roots or pine-cones, to your charcoal, then so much the better. Remember, do not start to cook until all the flames have gone and the embers are glowing red hot. Brush the fish in the grilling oil (see page 29) and shake off any excess – dripping oil causes flames that burn the fish rather than cook it. From time to time during the grilling, sprinkle herbs, such as rosemary and thyme, on to the embers.

Always have bits for your guests to nibble while they sip their apéritifs and wait for your charcoal-grilled masterpiece. Arrange to have a hot plate at hand to keep the food warm while you complete the cooking. All small whole fish lend themselves well to barbecueing, especially red mullet and sardines, as well as octopus, langoustines (Dublin Bay prawns), large prawns, anchovies, herrings, mackerel, tuna steaks, sprats, trout, pilchards and perch. Always remove all fins and scales from the fish, but never the skin — the crispy burnt skin is part of the joy of charcoal grilling and it protects the flesh from drying out. There is nothing worse than overcooked fish.

ESSENTIAL UTENSILS

1 Fish slice
2 Scissors for dealing with fins
3 Spatula
4 Filleting knife
5 12 in (30.5 cm) cook's knife for lobsters, etc.
6 Blunt knife for scaling
7 Fish-shaped grip for grilling large fish
8 Fish grip to sandwich small fish for grilling (sardines, for example)
9 Griddle
10 Ramekins
11 Steamer
12 Terrine mould
13 Bain-marie
14 Fish kettle/*turbotière*
15 Barbecue

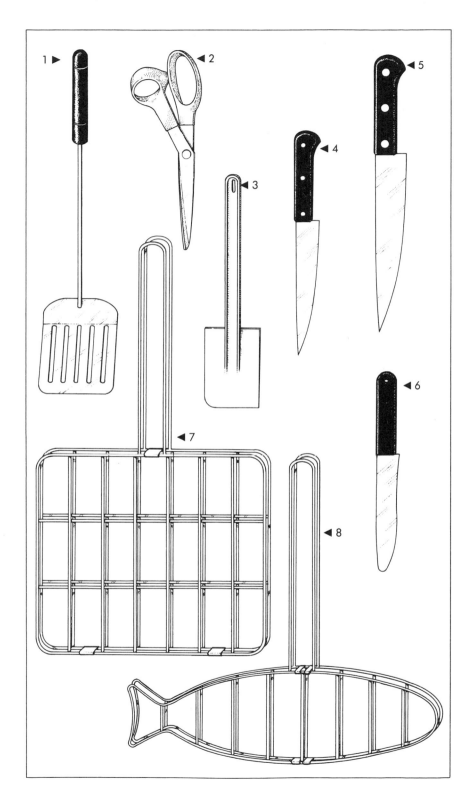

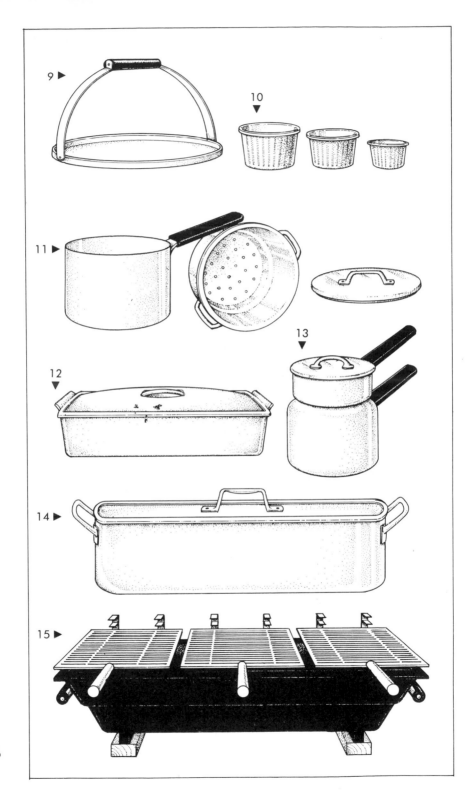

9 ▶

10 ▼

11 ▶

12 ▼

13 ▼

14 ▶

15 ▶

The sauces and flavoured butters that I have included in this section are just a few of the many ways of garnishing fish, and although they are relevant to the recipes in this book, they can be applied to many other fish or dishes. You can freeze the butters, enabling you to serve them at will, but the sauces must be made freshly, and should not swamp the fish – generally, 3 or 4 tablespoons will be sufficient per portion.

SAVOURY BUTTERS

A knob of any one of the following butters will cheer up the simplest piece of fish. Just roll the prepared butter in the shape of a sausage, wrap in grease-proof paper or foil and pop into the fridge or freezer for use as and when desired.

Anchovy Butter

6/7 anchovy fillets
4 oz (110 g) unsalted butter

Soften the butter and mash in the anchovy fillets.

Shrimp or Prawn Butter

2 oz (50 g) unshelled prawns or shrimps
Dash anchovy essence
Juice of 1 lemon
5 oz (150 g) unsalted butter

Grind the prawns or shrimps in a food processor. Add the anchovy essence, lemon juice and the softened butter. Whizz in the machine until smooth.

Lobster Butter

2 oz (50 g) lobster shell
Lobster roe
A little lobster meat
5 oz (150 g) unsalted butter

Grind the lobster shell in a food processor. Add the roe, the meat and the softened butter. Whizz until smooth.

Maître d'Hôtel Butter

8 oz (225 g) unsalted butter
4–5 tablespoons finely chopped parsley
Juice of 1 or 2 lemons to your taste

Soften the butter. Whizz all in a food processor until smooth.

And so it goes on. You can use fresh tarragon, smoked salmon or whatever you fancy to flavour butter.

Herb Oil for Grilling

30 black peppercorns
6 bay leaves
3 sprigs rosemary
4 sprigs thyme
4 red chillis
4/5 sage leaves
½ teaspoon fennel seeds
20 coriander seeds
Best quality olive oil

Stuff all the ingredients into a 1 litre wine bottle, cover with the olive oil, whack in the cork and leave for a week or two, to use as and when you wish.

STOCKS

All-purpose Court Bouillon

1¼ pints (700 ml) water
1¼ pints (700 ml) dry white wine or dry cider
1 tablespoon white wine vinegar
1 large onion, unpeeled and studded with 3 or 4 cloves
2 carrots, sliced
1 large leek, cut into 4
Bouquet garni
2 slices lemon

Simmer all the above ingredients for 30 minutes or so and allow to cool and strain before use. After you have poached your fish in the bouillon it would be sensible to save the liquid in the fridge in case you decide to make a fish soup the next day.

Dashi (Japanese Fish Stock)

Dashi is a delicate fish and seaweed stock. Happily, you can buy a powdered version, which is not bad, from oriental markets and wholefood shops. But in case you want to make your own, here it is:

- 1 × 4 in (3 × 10 cm) square of kelp seaweed (*kombu*)
- 2 pints (generous litre) water
- ½ oz (15 g) flaked bonito fish (*katsuobushi*)
- 1½ teaspoons salt
- 1 teaspoon Japanese soya sauce (*shoyu*)

Rinse and dry the seaweed. Then bring to the boil in the water and remove the seaweed. Pop in the fish and leave it to steep in the water, just as if you were making tea, for two or three minutes. Strain carefully and add the salt and soya sauce.

Simple Fish Stock

- 2 lb (scant kg) fish trimmings, bones, head, etc.
- 1 onion, chopped
- 1 carrot, chopped
- Celery leaves, or a leek, chopped
- 1 tablespoon peppercorns
- ¼ pint (150 ml) dry white wine
- 1 bouquet garni
- 1¾ pints (1 litre) water

Cover all the ingredients with the water and bring to the boil. Simmer for 30 minutes.

Strain through muslin or a very fine sieve and taste. If it is too bland, return to the heat and reduce until the flavour pleases you.

SAUCES

Aioli

- 8 cloves garlic
- 2 egg yolks
- ¾ pint (400 ml) good olive oil
- Juice of 1 lemon
- Salt and pepper

You should really crush the garlic in a pestle and mortar; then, with a whisk, stir in the egg yolks. Then you stir away madly, while you dribble the olive oil in until you have a thick, yellow mayonnaise. Last, you stir in the lemon juice and salt and pepper to taste.

Or you can put all the ingredients into a food processor, except for the olive oil, turn it on and pour in the oil, slowly but evenly, while the eggs and garlic are whizzing around. It will not be as good, but much quicker.

Béchamel Sauce (White Sauce)

2 oz (50 g) butter
3 tablespoons flour
17 fl oz (500 ml) milk
Salt and pepper
1 slice onion
1 bay leaf
1 slice carrot
1 sprig parsley
1 pinch grated nutmeg

Melt the butter and stir in the flour. Cook gently for 2 or 3 minutes without burning. In a separate pan, bring the milk to the boil with all the ingredients, except for the flour and butter, and leave to stand for 5 minutes. Strain. Pour the milk into the cooked flour and butter over a low heat, stirring all the while with a whisk. Simmer gently for 20 minutes or so, whisking occasionally until you have a thick creamy sauce.

Beurre Blanc Sauce

6 oz (175 g) unsalted butter
2 shallots, finely chopped
¼ pint (150 ml) dry white wine and white wine vinegar, mixed 60/40 in favour of wine
Salt and pepper

Cut up the butter into walnut-sized pieces. Boil the white wine and vinegar and shallots and reduce to a little over 2 tablespoons. Strain into another pan and, over a low heat, add the butter nut by nut, whisking furiously, until you have a smooth, creamy sauce. Don't stop whisking until you have. Add the seasoning.

Crayfish Sauce

18 oz (500 g) crayfish (or small langoustines, or at a pinch largish prawns)
3 tablespoons Cognac
18 fl oz (500 ml) fish stock (see page 30)
½ tablespoon flour
2 oz (50 g) unsalted butter
Salt and pepper
3 tablespoons double cream
2 egg yolks

Blanch the fish in boiling water for 2 or 3 minutes. Separate the tail meat intact and set aside for use as a garnish with a mousse or a poached fish, as desired.

Grind the shells in the liquidiser and cook in butter, adding the Cognac and the fish stock. Simmer for 10 minutes or so.

Cream the flour and butter together with your fingers and stir into the stock to thicken. Check for taste, and add salt and pepper. Stir in the cream and bubble the sauce up a little. Now turn off the heat, and straightaway whisk in the egg yolks vigorously.

Strain the sauce through a sieve or muslin to eliminate the shell pieces and serve at once. This sauce, because of the egg yolks, cannot be easily reheated.

Hollandaise Sauce (the quick and easy way)

Cookery writers and chefs of yesterday terrified the living daylights out of people with their old wives' tales about egg liaison sauces. Ignore all this. And follow me.

1 ½ lb (700 g) unsalted butter
6 eggs
Juice of 1 lemon
Pepper

Melt the butter in a pan with a pouring lip. Put the egg yolks and whites with the lemon juice and pepper into a food processor and turn on. Pour the hot melted butter evenly into the whisking eggs until the sauce has thickened. To keep warm, place over a pan of recently boiled water until ready to serve. And that, my little gastronauts, is that.

For variations you can add blanched sorrel leaves, finely chopped fresh mint and other herbs as you wish.

Mayonnaise

If you are to serve the mayonnaise straight, then you must use the best olive oil that you can afford, but if you intend to add herbs to it, as for tartare sauce, then use a blander corn or nut oil.

I have seen grown men and women burst into tears at the mystery of making this wonderful sauce. Here is the all-purpose, never-fail, Floyd technique:

6 whole eggs, at room temperature
Juice of 1 or 2 lemons
1 tablespoon wine vinegar
Salt and pepper
1¾ pints (1 litre) olive oil (or corn or nut oil) , at room temperature

Break the eggs into the food processor and add the other ingredients, except the oil. Turn the machine to maximum for 30 or 40 seconds, until the eggs are really foaming. Now pour the oil in evenly and slowly for a couple of minutes. If by any chance the mayonnaise is too thick, turn the machine on again at half speed and dribble some tepid water in.

I know, I know, you didn't need that amount. The point is you bottle the rest for the coming week.

My Mum's Parsley Sauce (the best in the world)

2 oz (50 g) butter
3 tablespoons flour
½ pint (300 ml) of the bouillon in which you have poached the fish
½ pint (300 ml) warm milk
Salt and pepper
6 tablespoons very finely chopped parsley
1 egg yolk
1 tablespoon double cream

Melt the butter in a pan. Stir in the flour and cook for about 3 minutes, being careful not to let it burn. Add the warm fish stock, stirring the while, then add the milk and salt and pepper. Simmer until a smooth sauce has been achieved. Add the parsley and simmer for a further 5 minutes. And just before you serve it, whisk in the egg yolk and cream rapidly.

● Obviously you can flavour this sauce as you wish – with, say, capers or mushrooms instead of the parsley.

● And if you had some lobster butter you could make *sauce cardinal*, by simply reducing the above sauce (without the parsley) by about a quarter and then adding 6 tablespoons of lobster butter, a chopped truffle or two and then whisking in the egg yolk and cream, as for the parsley sauce recipe.

● And, continuing in this theme, if you take the cardinal sauce without the lobster butter but substitute, say, 10 cooked mussels, a few fresh prawns and a couple of langoustines you have a *sauce Normande*. (Actually, leave in the lobster butter and you will have a *sauce super Normande*.)

Pink Sauce

This is a recipe that comes from the excellent Hotel St Hubert, St Saturnin d'Apt, in the Vaucluse. It is the perfect sauce for all cold fish cocktails.

2 egg yolks
2 tablespoons tomato ketchup
1 tablespoon bland oil (nut oil)
1 tablespoon olive oil
1 teaspoon mild Dijon mustard
4 tablespoons mild cream cheese (sometimes known as *fromage battue* or Petit Suisse)
Salt and pepper

Simply add all the ingredients to your food processor and whizz until you have a smooth, pourable consistency.

Rémoulade Sauce

½ pint (300 ml) mayonnaise, made with plain oil (see page 32)
½ tablespoon finely chopped parsley, tarragon, and basil
½ tablespoon chopped capers and gherkins
1 teaspoon mild mustard
2/3 anchovy fillets, finely chopped

Just mix all the ingredients into the mayonnaise.

Rouille

This classic fiery sauce is rarely made properly, often being presented as a spicy *aioli*. This is the authentic version, as given to me by a retired Provençal chef in a bar one evening.

2 large cloves garlic, peeled and finely chopped
2 red chillis (you can buy them fresh in certain greengrocers and supermarkets), chopped
Stale bread, soaked in water and squeezed out to the size of a large walnut
2–3 tablespoons olive oil

Grind the chopped garlic to a paste in a pestle and mortar – the quantity is too small for a food processor. Now pound in the nut of bread and the chopped chillis until smooth. Whisk in the olive oil until the mixture becomes like a smooth, shining red mustard.

Tartare Sauce

½ pint (300 ml) mayonnaise, made with plain oil (see page 32)
1 teaspoon finely chopped chives
1 teaspoon finely chopped capers
1 teaspoon finely chopped green olives
1 teaspoon finely chopped parsley
1 teaspoon finely chopped gherkins

Mix all the ingredients into the mayonnaise.

Fresh Tomato Sauce

1 onion, finely chopped
5 cloves garlic, crushed
4 tablespoons olive oil
1½ lb (700 g) ripe tomatoes, roughly chopped
1 tablespoon white sugar
2 tablespoons fruit-flavoured vinegar (raspberry for preference)
1 tablespoon chopped parsley
1 tablespoon chopped basil (I would rather you used dried than not put in any at all)
Salt and pepper
1 cup water

Sauté the onion and garlic in the olive oil until they are golden. Then add the rest of the ingredients and simmer gently for 30 minutes, at least. Liquidise and pass through a fine sieve. *Et voilà*. To be served hot or cold, as required.

Yoghurt Sauce

½ pint (300 ml) plain natural yoghurt (free range if possible)
3 tablespoons peeled and finely chopped cucumber
1 tablespoon chives, chopped
½ teaspoon concentrated mint sauce
Juice of ½ lemon
Salt and pepper

Mix together and chill.

In the days of coaching inns British sauces were a thing to be reckoned with. There was a time when Cumberland and Somersetshire sauce, to name but two, were beautifully prepared regional garnishes to tickle the palate of the dusty traveller. Then suddenly they invented lorries and factories and our gastronomic heritage was unceremoniously dumped into bottles and distributed, rich with stabilisers and colouring, from the central depot. The Americans, quick to exploit our weakness, dived in with ketchups and relishes. The unscrupulous continentals swiftly followed up with confections related only by name to the original recipes once they realised we eat with our eyes. British cooking had hit rock bottom. Even the great gravy had been sabotaged by boxes of powder and jars of black liquid.

My mum stuck out and still makes her gravy (the French call it *jus de rôti*) with the dripping from the meat and the water the vegetables were cooked in, thank goodness. But I digress.

Then came the colour supplements and Egon Ronay and *nouvelle cuisine* and suddenly we're all into sauce cooking again. Regrettably this often means pouring a gallon or two of cream over an otherwise perfectly good piece of fish or meat. It's significant that the French call *vinaigrette* a sauce, or even just two tablespoons of the roasting juices of a joint a sauce, and it's not poured over to disguise the taste of anything – it's to complement the flavours.

So please read my sauce recipes carefully – better a squeeze of lemon over a fillet of fish than a bucket of badly conceived liquid from a jar, no matter how grand the name. And don't swamp the food. Just a little goes a long way. Thank you.

A

ANCHOVY

The anchovy is seldom eaten fresh in Britain. It is more usually used in its filleted and olive-oiled state to flavour butter (see page 28) or for garnishing canapés or for making *anchoïade* – a paste with olive oil to spread on toast or celery. The very dullest piece of fish can be enlivened with a tablespoon of anchovy butter melted over it. But if you see some fresh ones, buy them and cook them like this:

Fresh Anchovies

Serves 4

> 2 lb (scant kg) fresh anchovies
> 5 oz (150 g) fresh breadcrumbs
> 3 oz (75 g) Parmesan cheese, grated
> 2 tablespoons parsley, chopped
> 1 teaspoon basil, chopped
> 1 teaspoon oregano, chopped
> 2 eggs
> Olive oil
> Salt and pepper

Dehead, gut and clean the fish. Rinse well under fresh water and dry with kitchen paper. Mix together the breadcrumbs, Parmesan and herbs. In another bowl, beat the two eggs with a little olive oil, salt and pepper as for an omelette.

Set the oven to gas mark 7/425°F/220°C. Smear a suitably attractive baking dish with olive oil and arrange a layer of anchovies in it. Brush these with more olive oil and cover with half of the breadcrumb and cheese mix. Now arrange another layer of fish and cover with the remainder of the mix. Sprinkle olive oil over the top and pour the beaten eggs over the lot. Cook for about 30 minutes.

Serve directly from the cooking dish with lots of fresh bread and crisp bitter salad – *frisée* (endive) and dandelion leaves with a garlic dressing would be good. And since this is an Italian dish, why not gulp down a few large glasses of chilled red wine with it?

If you can't be bothered with this recipe you can always barbecue the anchovies whole.

Anchoïade

Anchoïade is a quite brilliant savoury easily made by pounding (or liquidising) 2 small tins of anchovy fillets with 2 peeled cloves of garlic, a drop of vinegar and olive oil until you have a rough paste. Spread over pieces of cold toast, reheat in the oven for a moment and munch with your *apéritif*. Or spread it cold on batons of crisp celery.

AWOP-BOP-A-LOO-MOP-ALOP-BAM-BOOM (OR 2 AMERICAN GOLDEN OLDIES)

It is hard sometimes to take American food seriously, though they say New England lobsters are pretty good! Too many dishes are based upon the wholly unacceptable principles of quantity over quality and of convenience over care. There is also a heavy reliance on bottled sauces and canned foods. But if you are into Rock and Roll, as I am, you must remember the Fats Domino classic 'On the Bayou', where he sings of Jumbalaya crawfish pie and fillet gumbo.

And it was way down in Lousiana close to New Orleans
Back in the woods among the evergreens
Where Chuck Berry along with Little Richard, Fats and Elvis
Turned me onto Creole cooking.
So how about a midsummer morning party on the lawn:
A Rock and Roll gastronomic extravaganza
Washed down with what made Milwaukee famous.

And to Hell with the smirks from your orange-haired kids, who won't be up at this time on a Sunday morning after a night at the disco with Headache One Hundred.

Jumbalaya

Serves 6

It's one for the money:

1 tablespoon oil
4 slices bacon, chopped
1 onion, chopped
2 stalks white celery, chopped
12 oz (350 g) long grained rice, washed and dried
1 pint (570 ml) chicken stock
¼ teaspoon chilli powder
Salt and pepper
1 bay leaf
1 large green pepper, pithed, deseeded and chopped
14 oz (400 g) tin tomatoes
8 oz (225 g) clams or mussels, cooked and shelled
4 oz (110 g) cooked chicken, diced
8 oz (225 g) prawns, cooked and shelled (or crab or lobster)
1 tablespoon chopped parsley

Two for the show:
Heat the oil in a large pan and fry the bacon until crisp. Dry on kitchen paper. Add the onion, celery and rice to the oil and cook for 3 or 4 minutes, until the oil has coated all the grains of rice. Pour in the stock, with the seasonings and bay leaf, cover the pan and simmer gently for 10 minutes or so. Now add the green pepper, the tomatoes and their juice and simmer again, stirring occasionally, for another 5 minutes.

Three to get ready:
Stir in the shellfish, chicken and bacon pieces and simmer again for another 5 or 6 minutes, or until the rice is cooked and the last ingredients are heated through.

Now go go go:
Dish up on hot plates, sprinkle with parsley and eat with hot garlic bread.

And
Don't you
Step on my blue suede shoes.

Make Clam Chowder to start the festivities with:

Clam Chowder

Serves 6

4 oz (110 g) salt pork, diced
Oil for cooking
1 onion, chopped
4 tomatoes, skinned and chopped
3 potatoes, cut into ½ in (1 cm) cubes
Salt and pepper
½ teaspoon thyme
1 small bottle tomato juice
1 pint (570 ml) water
1 lb (450 g) fresh clams, without shells (it is all right to buy a tin of clams and use the juice as well)
¼ teaspoon cayenne, for garnish
6 tablespoons double cream, for garnish

Fry the salt pork in oil till crisp. Tip the oil into a soup pan and reserve the pork.
Fry the chopped onion in the soup pan until soft, not burnt, then add the tomatoes, potatoes, tomato juice, water, thyme, salt and pepper

and bring to the boil. Simmer until the potatoes are tender but not mushy. Stir in the clams and their juice, and the pork pieces, and simmer for another 5 minutes. Serve garnished with a tablespoon of double cream and a pinch of cayenne in each soup bowl.

You might like to steady your nerves and tummy with a shot of Bourbon on the rocks before moseying on down to the table.

B

BASS

This magnificent firm-fleshed fish for me is king. Far superior to even a good salmon. It is versatile – you can steam it, bake it, grill it, use it in *la bourride* (see page 45) and, thinly sliced, it can take pride of place in a Japanese *sashimi* (see page 69). The only trouble is that it is expensive and sometimes difficult to obtain – mainly because Chinese chefs are prepared to get up early to buy the lot to make Bass with Spring Onion and Ginger (see page 43). (If ever you go to fish markets, sidle up to a Chinese person and watch him shop. You will learn a thing or two.)

And, of course, the French gastronaut will travel miles and pay the earth to eat the classic bass dish *Loup de Mer au Fenouil*, especially in the Midi where waiters, with a glittering bass on a bed of flaming fennel stalks held high, glide like matadors between the packed tables of corpulent shirt-sleeved Marseilles bankers. And oh, the scents and aromas are too heady for words.

And this is how you cook it:

For 4, you will need a scaled, cleaned and gutted fresh bass of at least 2 lb (scant kg). Cut incisions on both sides and rub in coarse salt and black pepper. Inside the fish, put some more salt and some fresh fennel fronds and rub the whole fish with olive oil – not too much because you don't want drops spilling into the charcoal grill, causing flames and damaging the fish.

You will also need a really well-made charcoal grill (of course, use the electric one in the kitchen if you really have to), a bundle of dried fennel stalks and a large glass of *eau de vie*, Cognac or Armagnac. Also, since you must drink in style, why not a white Hermitage to share with your carefully chosen guests.

While you are standing around the charcoal, inhaling the delicious smell of the bass gently grilling, you may sip a heavily iced *pastis* instead of the usual G & T.

As the bass is cooking, and you should turn it over carefully at least once, place the bundle of dried fennel stalks on a long dish and above that fabricate a raised wire griddle on which to place the grilled fish. This done, pour the alcohol over the fish and fennel and set it alight. When the flames have died down, the bass will have absorbed the flavour of both and is ready to serve. You might like to pour a little melted butter over each portion, but no other sauce is necessary. The newest of new potatoes and a simple salad dressed with nut oil make a fine accompaniment. Follow with some strong goat's cheese or Roquefort and then some fresh raspberries or a sorbet and you will have enjoyed a sumptuous feast redolent of sun-drenched Provence.

Bass in White Wine

Serves 4

1 bass, about 2 lb (scant kg)
1 small onion, cut into fine rings
1 sprig fresh thyme
1 bay leaf
4 sprigs parsley
1 clove
Salt, pepper and nutmeg
½ pint (300 ml) white wine
4 oz (110 g) butter

Scale and gut the fish, wash well and dry it. Butter a shallow baking dish with some of the butter, saving the rest for the sauce.

Set the oven to gas mark 6/400°F/200°C. Spread the onion rings over the dish and lay the fish on them. Add all the herbs, spices and seasonings and pour in the wine. Cover with aluminium foil and bake for 30 minutes – be careful not to overcook it.

Take the fish from the oven and keep warm on a serving dish. Meanwhile strain the juices through a sieve into a saucepan over a medium heat and reduce until you have about 4 good tablespoons of liquid. Turn the heat down very low and add the rest of the butter, little by little, stirring all the time until the sauce thickens and becomes creamy. Incidentally this sauce is no more or no less than a *buerre blanc*, see page 31. But doesn't it seem less terrifying when described this way? To be a good cook you don't need the elitist threats of the colour supplements – just common sense and taste or, as *we* say – *élan*! (Hope you see the joke.) Pour the sauce over the fish and serve at once.

Boiled potatoes are all you need to accompany this splendid dish – use the money that you would have spent on vegetables to buy a better-than-usual white wine.

Ric Stein's Baked Bass
(From the Seafood Restaurant, Padstow)

Serves 4

1 bass, about 2 lb (scant kg)
Salt and pepper
Juice of 1 lemon
4 oz (110 g) butter
1½ lb (700 g) celery, carrot, and turnips, cut into thin batons 2 in (5 cm) long
9 fl oz (250 ml) white wine
Hollandaise or sorrel sauce (see page 32)

Scale, gut and clean the fish. Dry and rub well with salt, pepper and lemon juice, inside and out. Set the oven to gas mark 7/425°F/220°C.

Stir-fry the mixed vegetables in half of the butter for 8 minutes. Stuff the bass with the vegetables; lay the excess vegetables in a baking dish and place the bass on top. Add the white wine and the remaining butter, cover with aluminium foil and bake for about 30 minutes.

Place a portion of fish in the centre of each plate. Cover with hollandaise or sorrel sauce and arrange the vegetable batons, fan-like, around the fish.

Bass with Spring Onion and Ginger

Serves 4

1 bass, about 2¼ lb (1.3 kg)
Juice of 1 lemon

For the marinade:
1 tablespoon soya sauce
1 tablespoon cornflour
1 tablespoon rice wine or dry sherry
¼ teaspoon powdered ginger
Salt and pepper

For the sauce:
½ fl oz (15 ml) chicken stock
2 tablespoons rice wine or dry sherry
1 teaspoon sugar
Salt
½ tablespoon ginger, finely grated
2 leeks, white parts only, very finely sliced in roundels
6 tablespoons bland oil
4 spring onions, cut in quarters lengthways

Scale, gut, clean and wash the fish. Dry it well. Salt it and bathe in lemon juice for 10 minutes on each side.

Cut some incisions on each side of the bass and turn it over in the marinade several times during a 15-to-20-minute period.

Prepare the sauce by mixing the chicken stock with the sherry, sugar and a pinch of salt. Cook the fresh ginger and leeks gently in the oil for 10 minutes and put to one side, saving the oil to cook the bass.

Now fry the fish gently for 3 minutes on each side. Add the sauce mixture and the leeks, ginger and spring onions. Cover the pan with a lid and continue cooking gently for another 15 minutes.

BOUILLABAISSE

The pundits say that *bouillabaisse* does not travel, mainly because you cannot obtain the right fish for authenticity. And certainly I agree that it is hard to recapture the scent of the hot Marseilles streets, the whiff of petrol and Gauloises that waft around you as you sit under a blue *bâche* on the freshly washed terrace of a neat restaurant humming with controlled hysteria and excitement.

I reckon, however, that it is worth giving it a whirl; so close your eyes and think yourself back to France with this little recipe.

The Classic Bouillabaisse

Serves 6–8

2 large onions, finely chopped
5 ripe tomatoes, chopped
4 cloves garlic, crushed
1 leek, finely chopped
1 fl oz (25 ml) olive oil
1 tablespoon orange zest
1 sprig fennel
1 sprig thyme
4 pints (2.3 litres) boiling water
2 sachets saffron
5 lb (2.3 kg) mixed fish, which can include:
  John Dory
  Bass
  Gurnard
  Wrasse
  Dogfish
  Small, soft-shelled crabs
  Saith
  Weever fish
Salt and pepper
1 pot *rouille* (see page 34)
1 pot *aioli* (see page 30)
2 lb (scant kg) plain boiled potatoes

In a large pan, fry the onions, leek, garlic and tomatoes in the olive oil until golden. Then add the thyme, fennel and orange zest, mix in well and cook for a further 5 minutes.

Make sure the water is boiling furiously in readiness for the next phase – the boiling water, when mixed with the olive oil and vegetables, will liaise and thicken the resulting soup, which is essential for this dish.

Add the boiling water to the olive oil and vegetables over a high heat, whisking furiously for a minute or two, until the sauce thickens noticeably. Maybe add another slurp of olive oil at this time and keep boiling until you have the right consistency.

Add the fish – if they are unequal in size, start with the biggest first so that they all cook evenly. Season with salt and pepper, add the saffron and simmer until cooked – say, 10 or 15 minutes.

Lift the fish carefully from the sauce and remove the skin and bones. Arrange it in an attractive, shallow dish, and moisten with a cupful or two of the strained sauce. Strain the remainder of the sauce into a tureen and serve as a soup garnished with *rouille* and *aioli*. Then eat the fish with boiled potatoes and more *aioli*.

LA BOURRIDE

For me *la bourride* is one of the greatest dishes of Provence, and far superior to the *bouillabaisse* which cookery writers and tourists alike wax over a little too lyrically for my liking. Too often on the Côte, bouillabaisse comes from some frozen packet of Spanish origin. Even the French buy it without complaint, such is its reputation. I have eaten *bouillabaisse* that has varied from a stale fish soup to something quite excellent. But for me *la bourride* is *the* fish dish.

The best that I ever ate was at the Restaurant Michel in Marseilles. It was one of those formica, stainless steel and glass restaurants, which without the patina of frenetic style that the French call *élan* would have been a tasteless mish-mash.

A tense calm was imposed by the blue-suited, tinted-spectacled manager with the air of a minor villain from *The French Connection*. Purple-nosed matelots in *tricots* and cut-off wellingtons struggled with baskets of still flapping fish and creaking crustaceans, whilst serene Roman-faced waitresses, bristling in starched white overalls like a band of culinary sisters of mercy, smiled sweetly as they dispensed crystal goblets of kir.

I sat alone at a vast white table with heavy silver and shining glass and broke golden bread, still warm, into a mountain of ochre-coloured *aioli*, watching the Chinese cooks flashing silently around the kitchen. I sucked greedily at a plate of pink prawns and felt no guilt at drinking a bottle of *cassis* with them until a troupe of sisters arrived bearing plates and bowls.

A whole poached bass was swiftly skinned and the fillet placed on a large white plate, a lobster in two halves on either side, then covered with thick yellow sauce.

'Bon appetit, M'sieur.'

'You bet,' I said. And spread some more *aioli* on the dish.

An hour later I tried the chocolate cake, and drained my *marc* at 4.15. Too late, I realised, I'd ignored the cheese . . . .

The recipe for *la bourride* that follows is based on the dish that I ate that day at Michel's and on many subsequent visits thereafter.

NB   People will tell you that shellfish should never appear in *la bourride* – Michel and I disagree.

La Bourride Marseillaise

Serves 4

2 live lobsters
4 fillets thick, white fish (bass, monkfish, turbot, brill, etc.)
7 fl oz (200 ml) double cream
½ pint (300 ml) *aioli* (see page 30)

For the stock:
2 pints (generous litre) water
Fish head and bones
2 slices lemon
2 leeks, chopped
1 carrot, sliced
1 bay leaf

Simmer the stock for 20 minutes and strain. Into the strained stock place the lobsters, bring to the boil with a lid on the pan, reduce heat and simmer for 20 minutes.

Remove the lobsters and keep warm while you poach the fillets of fish in the same stock for, say, 15 minutes, depending on their thickness.

Cut the lobsters in half and arrange on a large serving dish with the fish fillets – keep warm.

Now reduce the remaining stock to about a third of its original volume and, over a low heat, stir in the cream. Carefully whisk half of the *aioli* into the sauce, stirring over a low heat until the sauce takes on the colour and consistency of custard. Pour over the fish and serve at once.

Don't forget, lots of fresh bread to mop up the sauce, maybe some plain boiled potatoes, too. And another bowl of *aioli* for the gluttons.

Don't be afraid of drinking a chilled red wine with this.

BREAM

The bream is a fine, delicate fish easily found in Britain, but of course little used. It is highly esteemed in France and Spain. Two varieties are available here, the black bream and the red. The red bream makes better eating.

Bream with Fresh Herbs

Serves 4

1 bream, at least 2 lb (scant kg)
Salt and pepper
1 sprig fresh thyme
1 bayleaf
3 spring onions, chopped
3 tablespoons oil
7 fl oz (200 ml) white wine
2 fronds fresh fennel, chopped
1 tablespoon chopped parsley

Scale, gut, clean and wash the bream and then dry it carefully. Set the oven at gas mark 7/425°F/220°C.

With some of the oil, grease an ovenproof dish. Salt and pepper the bream inside and out and put the thyme and bay leaf inside the fish. Pop the fish into an oven dish, add the spring onions and the rest of the oil and cook for 10 minutes.

After 15 minutes, add the white wine, fennel and parsley and cook for a further 15 minutes.

BRILL

The brill is less well known (and cheaper) than the turbot but a pretty good fish all the same. My mum poaches it whole in a court bouillon (see page 29), then skins and fillets it and serves it with boiled carrots and a super parsley sauce (see page 33).

Brill with Rhubarb

I felt so sorry for the British rhubarb industry after hearing Derek Cooper's report on its declining fortunes on Radio 4's *Food Programme* that I thought I would include this dish to help demand.

Serves 4

> 1 oz (25 g) butter
> 4 fillets of brill
> 1 ¼ pints (700 ml) court bouillon (see page 29)
> 6 sticks rhubarb, cooked without sugar, puréed and kept warm
> ¼ pint (150 ml) double cream
> Salt and pepper

Butter a baking dish and lay the fillets on it. Cover with the bouillon and seal with the aluminium foil. Bake in the oven at gas mark 6/400°F/200°C for about 15 minutes.

Lift the fillets from the bouillon and place them on a serving dish. Cover with the rhubarb purée and keep warm in the oven.

Take the bouillon in which you cooked the fish and reduce it over a fierce flame until less than ½ pint (300 ml). Add the cream and cook for a further 1 minute, add salt and pepper to taste. Pour this sauce over the rhubarb-covered fillets and eat.

Brill Fillets in Tomato Sauce

Serves 4

> 4 fillets of brill, about 7 oz (200 g) each
> Juice of 1 lemon
> 1 ½ oz (40 g) butter
> 2 large onions, finely chopped
> 1 lb (450 g) tomatoes, skinned and pulped
> Salt and pepper
> Oil, for deep frying
> 3 tablespoons flour
> 4 fl oz (110 ml) dry sherry
> ¼ pint (150 ml) double cream
> Parsley for garnish, finely chopped

Rinse and dry the fillets and marinate in lemon juice for 30 minutes.

Melt the butter in a pan and sauté the onions until golden. Add the tomato, salt and pepper and cook gently for a further 15 minutes.

Heat the oil for deep frying to 370°F/187°C. Dredge the fillets in the flour and deep fry them for 2–3 minutes until golden. Remove from the oil, dry on a kitchen towel, and keep to one side.

Now add the sherry and cream to the tomato mixture and cook, gently, for 3 more minutes. Add the brill fillets and cook gently for a further 2 minutes. Serve the fillets on an elegant plate, anoint with the sauce and garnish with parsley.

Bass with Spring Onion and Ginger; *Over*: Aioli de Morue

C

CLAMS

They look like flat pebbles in between the piles of mussels and whelks on the French fish stalls. You can eat them raw like oysters, or grill them in the half-shell with garlic butter like snails, or murder them in clam chowder like our beloved transatlantic friends (see page 40) but if you do see some, here is a really simple dish to make in a hurry when you've impulsively bought some clams from the fishmonger and are then wondering what to do with them.

Clams with Pasta

Serves 4

12 clams per person (more if they are very small)
4 oz (110 g) smoked ham or rindless smoked streaky bacon, chopped
5 tablespoons olive oil
1 tablespoon chopped fresh basil
1 tablespoon finely chopped parsley
2 teaspoons tomato purée
1 tablespoon pine-nuts
Salt and pepper
Parmesan cheese, grated
Fresh pasta

Wash the clams under cold water and put them in a frying pan with 1 cup of water over a low heat until they start to open. As soon as they open, remove from the heat and extract the clams from the shells. Save 6 or 7 tablespoons of the clam juice.

In a large pan brown the bacon with all the olive oil for 1 or 2 minutes. Add all the other ingredients, except for the cheese. Add the clam juice that you have reserved and cook, stirring gently, over a low heat for 10 minutes or so.

5 minutes before the clams and sauce are ready, add the pasta to furiously boiling salted water and cook until *al dente* (firm to the bite). Strain and put into a serving dish. Add the cooked clams and sauce and gently toss. Accompany with a bowl of freshly grated Parmesan.

COD

One winter I lived on a boat in a Norwegian fjord and twice a week around dawn a retired sea captain, returning from fishing, would hammer on the hull and shout, 'Hey, English, wake up. I got you fish, you lazy boy!' He would be gone before I had pulled on my clothes and stumbled through the hatch. But the cod that he had thrown down was still flapping. What breakfasts we had. Cod fried in butter, black coffee and iced vodka!!

Cod Grilled with Anchovy Butter

Serves 4

4 good slices (not cutlets) of cod
Salt
2 tablespoons olive oil
4 oz (110 g) butter
Pepper
1 tablespoon capers in vinegar, finely chopped
1 tablespoon anchovy paste
Juice of ½ lemon

Switch on the grill – this may sound obvious, but too many people put their fish on to the tray and *then* turn it on. The grill must be at its hottest *before* you start to cook.

Wash and dry the fillets. Sprinkle them with salt and rub with oil. Cook the fillets for 3 or 4 minutes on each side.

In the meantime, soften the butter and add the capers, pepper, lemon juice and anchovy paste. Coat the (now cooked) fillets with the butter and serve at once. A pile of thinly sliced, deep-fried courgettes (which you have soaked in milk and dredged in flour) goes really well with this dish.

Cod Fillet in Yellow Bean Sauce

Before you start screaming, you can buy a tin or jar of yellow bean sauce from a Chinese supermarket. This dish makes an excellent meal for two or three or can be part of a larger Chinese banquet.

Serves 2 or 3

1 lb (450 g) cod fillet, cut into 1 in (2.5 cm) cubes
1 or 2 tablespoons yellow bean sauce
3 tablespoons dark soya sauce
1 tablespoon rice wine or dry sherry
1 tablespoon white sugar
1 teaspoon fresh green chilli, seeded and cut into very fine rings
2 tablespoons oil

Mix all the ingredients, except the oil, in a bowl and marinade the fish for 1 hour. Heat the oil in a wok and stir-fry the fish on a medium heat for just a few minutes till golden and almost cooked. Add the marinade and continue cooking until the sauce has reduced, leaving the fish well coated and moist. Serve with steamed broccoli or *pak choi*.

COD, SALT

Salt cod hangs drying like ragged washing on the beaches of Spain and Portugal. In Norway it hangs from the eaves of boathouses. In France a dish of salt cod is *de rigueur* for the Christmas Eve feast (they mean fast), and absolutely essential for the *al fresco* village feasts of *Aioli* held throughout the Midi during summer. And the salt cod speciality of Nîmes, creamed salt cod, is the stuff that gives French lorry drivers a happy smile and pot-bellies as they waddle to their huge shiny trucks in the late afternoon. Reeking of garlic, they gun the motors and roar on down the RN 7 to dinner (and presumably discharge their load of artichokes or fish fingers at some Godforsaken hour in the early dawn).

In England it is reviled, although I enjoyed it poached in milk as a kid. We called it tea fish and often ate it for breakfast. My grandfather thought it suitable for soling shoes. But he was wrong.

It is mainly available in this country through delicatessens and West Indian shops or can be ordered from your fishmonger.

Brandade de Morue (Creamed Salt Cod)

Serves 6

2 lb (scant kg) plump salt cod
1¾ pints (1 litre) best olive oil
¼ pint (150 ml) double cream
3 cloves garlic, crushed
Juice of 1 lemon
1 tablespoon chopped parsley

Soak the cod overnight and rinse thoroughly in fresh water to eliminate the salt. Poach the fish gently in water until cooked. Remove all the skin and bones, and, while still warm, mince it very finely – a blender may make it a little stringy.

Put the minced cod into a saucepan over a low heat and have ready another pan with the olive oil in, slightly warm, and the cream close at hand. Ideally you need three hands for this operation, one to stir the cod constantly with a wooden spoon, a second to be slowly dripping in the oil and a third to be dripping in the cream. Ignore everyone else and keep stirring vigorously. You must stir and stir until you achieve the consistency of creamed mashed potato. Only then can you take a slurp from the glass on the work top (oh for a fourth hand).

Add the lemon juice, garlic and parsley, stirring the while, then tip into a prewarmed dish and eat immediately with triangles of fried bread and gallons of Provençal rosé.

Fit for soling shoes indeed!

Aioli de Morue (or A Feast of Salt Cod, Garlic Mayonnaise and Vegetables)

If you are ever driving through Provence and you see a banner draped across the village main street saying something such as *Fête Campagnard: Grand Aioli Monstre*, stop at once, go into the nearest bar and ask for a ticket. You will find yourself at long trestle tables in the village square, under the plane trees, with the town band thumping off key. Servants will bring you jugs of wine and huge bowls of garlic mayonnaise and salt cod. And the sky will be blue and clear and you will drink and eat far too much. But no blame attaches. Bacchus and the spirit of Brillat-Savarin will smile benignly on this day of days. And long after the memory has faded, you can recreate the feast on summer days in your own garden. You must invite at least 6 friends, of hearty appetite and thirst.

Serves at least 6; increase quantities all round as necessary

2½ lb (1.2 kg) salt cod
Aioli (see page 30): 1 pint (570 ml) serves 6 extravagantly
6 potatoes
12 carrots
12 small turnips
6 leeks
10 oz (275 g) whole green beans
6 hard-boiled eggs

Soak the cod overnight and rinse thoroughly to remove salt. Prepare the *aioli*. Cook all the vegetables, simply and separately in salted water.

While they are cooking, put the cod into cold water over a low heat and bring slowly to the boil. Once boiling, turn the heat down and simmer for 8 minutes. Then turn off the heat, cover the saucepan and check the vegetables.

Strain the cod, take off the skin and arrange with the strained vegetables on a large plate. Decorate with hard-boiled eggs. Serve the *aioli* separately.

In summer you can use other vegetables, for example asparagus, artichokes, broad beans, cauliflower, fennel, celery, etc.

With the older country people of Provence, *aioli* is not so much a meal as an event. A day long festival of *boules, pastis* and gourmandising, spiced with tall stories and jokes.

I was once invited by a retired farmer to his home for lunch. Be there at 11 am, he said. Until noon we played *boules* and drank home-made *pastis*, which is diabolically strong. Ten of us sat at a long table in the cool, shuttered gloom, barely able to see the dishes of eggs, potatoes, carrots, beans, artichoke hearts, small turnips, two wobbling blancmanges of *aioli* like small yellow mountains set at each end of the table, asparagus, leeks neatly tied in small bunches, a steaming plate piled high with cod and a huge *marmite* filled with snails. A litre bottle of iced red wine was at each place setting and we started to eat. By 2.30 the table was a ruin, the dishes empty. I pushed my chair back and stretched in a gastronomic stupor.

My hostess cleared the table and to my amazement relaid the place settings. I could hardly believe my eyes when she placed two smouldering legs of roast lamb before us. And a bath of *petits pois* stewed with lettuce and ham, and bottles of iced rosé.

'Eat, my friends,' she ordered, 'you are in Provence. This isn't France.'

Hard yellow nuggets of goat's cheese followed, then *katcha* (macerated goat cheese blended with *eau de vie* and olive oil), then bleeding red strawberries and plates of sugary biscuits, then coffee and *marc*, then cakes and champagne. . . .

Then someone said, 'The sun is off the courtyard. It's time for *l'apéritif* and a game of *boules*.'

It was 7 pm.

PS A delightful nibble with *apéritifs* can be served by cubing raw salt cod (about ¼ in/6 mm in size) and mixing with raw broad beans. Often served as a *tapa* in Spain, a cube of the salt cod and a broad bean should be popped into the mouth at the same time.

CRAB

It is a risky business to buy a precooked crab (and frozen crabmeat is out of the question), so buy live ones and cook them yourself. If possible, they should be cooked in seawater with a couple of tablespoons of extra salt added. So, simply pop your live crabs into cold salted water and bring to the boil. Immediately reduce the heat and gently simmer for 10 minutes. Then switch off the heat and leave the crabs in the water until cool.

To open the crab, first twist off the claws and legs (1). Then separate the body from the shell (2). Remember that as well as the brown and white meat in the body, you will discover a considerable amount of delicious flesh in the compartmentalised chine. The inedible parts of a crab are the lungs and the sac, which should be discarded (3). Crack the claws to remove the meat (4). Use the cleaned shell as a dish for the crabmeat (5,6).

Simple fresh crab served this way, with salad, lemon juice and a good mayonnaise (see page 32) is superb. I don't think that hot crab dishes with cheese sauces, etc., are really worth the trouble. If you ever come across spider crabs, snap them up. Cook them the same way, but only eat the claws, which are full of succulent meat, and use an *aioli* (see page 30) instead of mayonnaise.

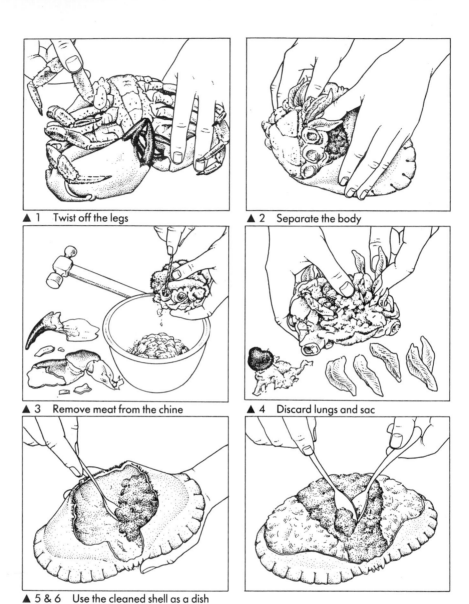

▲ 1   Twist off the legs

▲ 2   Separate the body

▲ 3   Remove meat from the chine

▲ 4   Discard lungs and sac

▲ 5 & 6   Use the cleaned shell as a dish

Potted crab

Serves 4–5

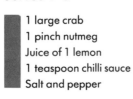

1 large crab
1 pinch nutmeg
Juice of 1 lemon
1 teaspoon chilli sauce
Salt and pepper

Take all the meat from the crab (which you have cooked yourself), and season well with the nutmeg, salt and pepper, lemon juice and chilli sauce. Mix these ingredients well together and pack into ramekins. Cover with melted butter and bake in a bain-marie, in a low oven, for 20 minutes.

When they are almost cool, top up the ramekins with clarified butter and allow to set.

While they are cooling, pop into the garden, lift a fresh crisp lettuce, wash and dry it and make a dressing of mild mustard, lemon juice, 1 teaspoon sugar, 1 tablespoon each of wine vinegar and olive oil. Check that the wine is cool, pull the garden table under the tree out of the sun, and tell your husband to stop messing around with your son's train set, and to present the chilled wine a bit smartish. Or you'll eat his potted crab!

D

DOGFISH

'Yuck,' I hear you howl, 'we're not eating dogfish!'

Well, I agree they look pretty dreadful and I am sure that my grandad (see Salt Cod, page 53) would be thrilled to know that you could use the rough skin of this fish for polishing wood, alabaster and even beaver hats. But they do make great eating. Indeed, the famed *bouillabaisse* needs it, as does the warm red-brown fish soup of the south coast of France. Anyway, you have probably already eaten it. Often the ubiquitous and anonymous fish and chips (where no actual species is named, I hasten to add to appease the honest purveyor of the great British identified frying object) is nothing more nor less than dogfish.

NB Dogfish is always sold skinned and cut into little logs.

Dogfish with a Piquant Tomato Sauce

Serves 4

> 4 logs of dogfish, about 5 oz (150 g) each
> Fish stock for poaching (see page 30)
> ¼ pint (300 ml) tomato sauce (see page 34)
> ½ tablespoon *harissa* or chilli sauce
> 1 tablespoon chopped basil
> 4 tablespoons cream
> Parsley for garnish, chopped
> Salt and pepper

Poach the dogfish for 10–15 minutes in the stock. Remove and keep warm.

Into another pan put the tomato sauce with 6 tablespoons of the stock, the *harissa* or chilli sauce, and basil. (*Harissa*, a chilli paste from North Africa, is an enormously useful ingredient which you'll find in good delicatessens and health food shops.) Bring to the boil and reduce by about one-third, or until you have the consistency of runny custard.

Coat the fish with the sauce and pour 1 spoonful of the cream in thin wavy lines over each portion; decorate with parsley. Accompany with small fried potatoes.

E

EEL, CONGER

For my taste, hot conger eel is too sweet and I never liked it until I ate it cold with salad in the garden of a small restaurant in Saumur, on the Loire. Actually it is the only meal that I have ever liked in that area of France. I felt then that many of the chefs around the region would benefit enormously by reading Elizabeth David's *French Provincial Cooking*!

Cold Conger and Salad

Serves 4

4 firm round cutlets of eel
1 ¼ pints (700 ml) fish stock (see page 30)
Rémoulade sauce (see page 34)

For the salad:
Heart of 1 *frisée* (endive)
1 lb (450 g) cooked asparagus
4 tomatoes, finely sliced and marinated in raspberry vinegar and finely chopped basil
2 hard-boiled eggs, cut into halves

Poach the eel for 15 minutes in the stock and allow it to cool. Remove and strain the fish. Take off the skin.

Lay the cutlets on a bed of *frisée* and coat with the rémoulade sauce. Decorate with the tomatoes, asparagus and eggs.

You might follow this with a dish of piping hot new potatoes tossed in olive oil, wine vinegar and coarse salt.

EEL, FRESHWATER

If you happen to be a freshwater eel fisherman, or find yourself stranded on the river Loire in your yacht, penniless, and a mad fisherman in a bar gives you a sack of squirming eels in exchange for your last bottle of duty-free whisky, this recipe from the great Curnonsky (née Maurice Edmond Sailland at 3 am, 12 October 1872, in Angers) might be of interest to you. Unfortunately it certainly didn't interest my fellow crew members on the good yacht *Flirtie*, who would have preferred a steak any day.

To skin an eel you should suspend it with string around the head from a convenient hook. Make an incision all around, enough for you to get a good grip (1), and then work the skin free and pull sharply downwards, pulling the skin off like a sheath (2).

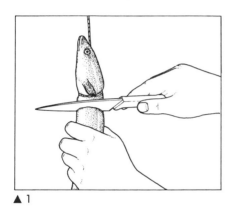

▲ 1

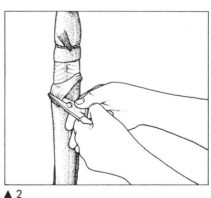

▲ 2

Eel Stewed in Red Wine

Serves 6

1 onion, finely chopped
2 carrots, chopped small
White of 1 leek, chopped small
6 oz (175 g) butter
2 bottles good red wine (if you won't drink it, don't cook with it)
1 sprig fresh thyme
1 bay leaf
2 sprigs parsley
Salt and pepper
20 small onions (you can buy them frozen if you can't be bothered to peel fresh ones)
2¾ lb (1.6 kg) fresh eel, skinned and cut into finger-length pieces
2 fl oz (50 ml) Cognac
Pinch nutmeg
2 oz (50 g) flour

To make the sauce, fry the chopped onion, carrot and leek in 2 oz (50 g) of the butter until golden. Add the red wine, thyme, bay leaf and parsley, and cook gently for 1 hour. Add the salt and pepper.

Prepare the garnish by frying the whole small onions in some butter until golden. Add a cup of the wine sauce and simmer until they are cooked. Put on one side.

Place the eels in a saucepan and strain the rest of the wine sauce over. Add the Cognac, a little nutmeg and bring to the boil. Simmer for about 20 minutes.

To finish, make a roux with 2½ oz (60 g) butter and 2 oz (50 g) flour. Lift the cooked eel pieces from their pan and keep them warm in a serving dish. Strain the sauce on to the roux, bubbling the while until it thickens, stirring with a whisk to eliminate lumps. Arrange the whole onions around the eel and strain the thickened sauce over the lot. Eat at once and drink a bottle of the same wine you cooked it in.

Or would you rather have a steak?

F

FISH SOUP

It is hard to see into the restaurant at Courthezon. The windows are screened in fly-blown plastic strips and are pasted with vivid posters advertising *boules* festivals and circuses. It is in one of those streets that has two or three dogs dozing on the railway track that runs alongside shuttered houses, crumbling pale blue and yellow under a brilliant sun.

The plane trees are neat but dusty and there is a hum of machinery from a factory behind the station. The owner of the restaurant looks up and down the deserted street, pecking into the dry heat like a scrawny parrot. A huge red truck grinds past and darkens the cool restaurant like thunder clouds. A crack and hiss of air-brakes startles me, but the dogs don't move. I sip my *pastis* while a waitress places bread and wine on the empty formica tables in the cool dining-room. She puts a litre of iced red wine, the bottles glinting with beads of condensation, between each place setting and in the kitchen three sisters, in white overalls and with grey hair stretched into neat buns above their pink faces, are softly stirring simmering cauldrons.

In the still noon, the town clock begins to strike a neat pinging sound, as if from a distance. The street fills with swarthy men shouting and jostling, a rabble of multi-coloured T-shirts and jeans swamps the restaurant. The din is shattering. Before the clock strikes twelve, every table is full and big fingers rip into loaves of bread and thirsty lips suck down the wine from unbreakable tumblers. And the waitress, without a word, delivers tureens of steaming brown fish soup. You fill your bowl with grated cheese and a dollop of red *rouille* before you ladle in the soup. And eat your way into the afternoon.

There is no soup like the Provençal soup. The creamy concoctions of Normandy leave me cold, and the bowls of white sauce packed with pre-cooked prawns, scallops and old mussels that all too often passes for fish soup in Britain leave me speechless.

Before making fish soup it is a good idea to have a word with your friendly fishmonger because, unless you live near a proper market, you will have difficulty in getting the right fish. Order it ahead; it is a pretty expensive dish to prepare so you might as well go the whole hog and do it properly, by making the soup the central feature of the meal. Iced dry rosé or iced weak red wine should be drunk in great quantities, as well as lots of really fresh white bread. Offer people kir or *pastis* as an *apéritif* and get them into the southern frame of mind.

Floyd's Fish Soup

Will make a feast for 6

2¼ lb (1.3 kg) mixed fish, which must include:
Gurnard or red mullet
Small soft-shelled crabs
Conger eel
John Dory
A handful of langoustines
A piece of dogfish
2 leeks, chopped
2 onions, chopped
2 large ripe tomatoes, chopped
2 large cloves garlic, crushed
Olive oil for frying
4 pints (2.3 litres) water
1 teaspoon orange peel zest
1 bay leaf
1 frond fresh fennel
Salt and pepper
4 oz (110 g) small vermicelli
1 sachet saffron
Rouille (see page 34)
Aioli (see page 30)
5 oz (150 g) Gruyère cheese, grated

Cut, wash and clean the fish. Chop into pieces about 2½ (6 cm) long — head, bones and all. Fry the leeks, tomatoes, onions and garlic in oil until soft but not brown. Add the water to the vegetables and bring to the boil. Now add all the fish, the bay leaf, fennel and orange zest and cook rapidly for another 15 minutes.

Remove the fish and allow the soup to simmer gently. Meanwhile, crush or grind the fish in a liquidiser and return it to the soup. Stir it well and strain the lot through a fine sieve into another pan. Throw away any bits left in the sieve. The soup should be smooth, not lumpy, and have no bones or bits of shell in it.

Bring this strained soup to the boil, add salt and pepper to taste and add the vermicelli and saffron. Once the vermicelli is cooked, the soup is ready. (It is sensible to make the soup well in advance otherwise you will be exhausted by the time you eat it – in which case do not add the vermicelli until just before you serve the soup, otherwise it will have swelled and become glutinous, overwhelming the soup.)

Let your guests add their own *rouille*, according to their taste, and help themselves to grated cheese, which they also stir in. Tell them to spread the *aioli* on bread and dunk it in.

PS When you make this fabulous dish I would like you to know that I am always available if one of your guests fails to turn up!

G

GREY MULLET

The grey mullet, no relation to the smaller red mullet, is grand for baking and less good for poaching. The grey mullet is a dirty eater and has a huge and often unpleasant gut. It must be thoroughly cleaned and washed. It must also be carefully scaled, as the scales are large and indigestible.

Grey Mullet with Cream and Red Peppers

Serves 4

1 grey mullet, about 2¼ lb (generous kg)
Salt
Juice of 1 lemon
2 oz (50 g) butter
2 oz (50 g) smoked bacon, diced
2 red peppers, cleaned and cut into fine strips
1 large onion, finely chopped
4 ripe tomatoes, skinned and pulped
6 fl oz (175 ml) double cream
1 tablespoon prepared mild mustard

Scale, gut, clean, wash and dry the fish. Season inside and out with salt and lemon juice. Set the oven to gas mark 7/425°F/220°C.

Butter a baking dish with half of the butter and put in the mullet. Cover the fish with all the bacon and half of the peppers. Put the rest of the peppers, the onions and tomatoes around the fish and dot little pieces of the remaining butter on the fish itself. Put into the oven for about 20 minutes. Baste the fish with the cooking juices from time to time.

Mix the cream and mustard together thoroughly. Pour over the fish and cook for another 10 minutes.

Boiled or pilau rice would be a good accompaniment.

GURNARD

In Britain, gurnards are largely used as lobster and crab bait, whereas in France you will often find them in fish soups and *bouillabaisse*. In Spain and Latin America they are delicious cooked in a piquant tomato sauce, and as long as you fillet the fish well (they are a bit bony) you will be well rewarded for having the sense to buy this cheap fish.

Mexican Gurnard

Serves 4

2 fl oz (50 ml) olive oil
1 large onion, finely chopped
2 cloves garlic, finely chopped
1 ½ lb (700 g) fresh ripe tomatoes, peeled, liquidised and strained of pips
6 stoned green olives, halved
6 stoned black olives, halved
2 fresh red chillis, finely chopped
8 small gurnard fillets
Seasoned flour
Butter to cook
Juice of 1 lime

Heat the oil and sauté the onion and garlic till golden. Add the tomato, olives and chillis and simmer for 20 minutes.

Meanwhile, dredge the gurnard fillets in the flour and fry in the butter till they are browned and cooked. Place on a serving dish, squeeze over the lime juice, cover with sauce, and tuck in.

H

HADDOCK

I hope the haddock won't be offended when I call it one of those useful, all purpose fish. Although not as splendid as the cod, it can be used in the same ways and is excellent dipped in a good batter and deep fried.

When poached, the firm, flaky flesh, free of skin and bone, is grand for making a simple gratin – easily produced by pouring a cheese flavoured béchamel sauce (see page 31) over the fish and popping under a grill till the sauce turns golden and the fish heats through.

Haddock Cooked in Milk

Serves 4

1 ¾ lb (810 g) haddock
1 ¾ pints (1 litre) milk

For the sauce:
4 oz (110 g) butter
Juice of 1 lemon
3 tablespoons capers
Salt and pepper

Wash and dry the haddock. Put the fish into a saucepan and cover with milk. Bring to the boil and then simmer for 10 minutes.

Meanwhile, melt the butter and add the lemon juice, capers, salt and pepper and keep hot.

Lift the haddock from the milk with a sieve and pop on to a plate – you don't use the milk. Pour over the sauce and put those nasty dreams you had about fish and chip shops quite out of mind.

Chinese Fish Soup with Haddock Fillets

Serves 4

1 lb (450 g) haddock fillets, in 4 pieces
1 ½ teaspoons sea salt
1 ½ teaspoons ground ginger
2 tablespoons vinegar
Vegetable oil for deep frying
1 ½ pints (900 ml) light chicken stock
½ teaspoon black pepper
1 ½ tablespoons soy sauce
2 tablespoons rice wine or dry sherry
5 tablespoons watercress leaves

Rub the fish with salt, ginger and half the vinegar and leave to marinate for at least 1 hour. Dry the fish and deep fry for 5 or 6 minutes, until the outsides are crisp but not burnt.

Bring the chicken stock to the boil and add the fish. Turn down the heat and add the pepper, soy sauce, the remaining vinegar, rice wine and the watercress leaves, and simmer for another 6 minutes or so.

HERRINGS

Surprise, surprise. The humble herring is back in fashion. Long regarded as a dish for the poor and needy, overfished by our more discerning neighbours and despised by the gastronaut, it has suddenly been decreed by the Great Authorities that we should eat them again. Britain must be the only country in the world that virtually needs an Act of Parliament passed to make us eat fish – or at least a massive plug on the *Jimmy Young Show*, which is practically the same thing.

Anyway, as a child I loved to eat a hot herring baked in vinegar, cloves and onions for supper on Saturday night, or a crisply fried herring for breakfast with doorsteps of warm, crusty bread and butter.

Herrings with Bacon

Serves 4

8 fresh herrings (as opposed to smoked or salted ones), about 5 oz (150 g) each
Juice of 2 lemons
Salt
2 tablespoons prepared mild mustard
16 rashers rindless streaky bacon
4 fl oz (110 ml) oil

Dehead, slit, clean, scale, wash and dry the herrings. Then, with forefinger and thumb inside the fish under the central spine, take out as many bones as you can without ripping the flesh.

Fold the fish out flat and brush the insides with lemon and sprinkle with salt. Next, spread a little mustard on each one, close the fish and wrap each in bacon, using a cocktail stick to hold the bacon in place.

Now cook the herrings in oil in a shallow frying pan for about 6 minutes on each side, until the bacon is golden and the herrings cooked. Do not have the oil too hot to begin with, or else the bacon will be cremated before the little old herrings are cooked.

Pat off excess fat with a paper tissue and tuck in, with a really fresh, crisp, mixed salad of raw fennel, tomatoes, red and white cabbage or any gutsy, crunchy combination of vegetables you fancy. And why not use this dish as an excuse to drink near frozen vodka or aquavit with lager chasers?

HAKE

In La Coruña, tired and emotional after a night on the town that had succeeded an exhilarating sail from Plymouth to that Spanish haven of bacchanalia, I was brought a plate of fish smothered in tomatoes, black olives and fried potatoes. Oh, I suppose there was garlic and olive oil, too. But despite the excitement of the occasion – my first meal in Spain following a terrifying voyage in the works yacht, hell of white water, waves with teeth like bananas, nothing on the clock but the maker's name, etc. – I really felt that hake, for that was the fish, could taste better than it did on that Sunday afternoon in La Coruña.

This recipe from Sonia Stevenson, of the famed Horn of Plenty restaurant in Tavistock, is a superb example of how to cook hake.

Sonia's Hake
(From the Horn of Plenty, Tavistock, Devon)

Serves 4

4 cutlets of hake
Salt and pepper
2 oz (50 g) butter
½ onion, finely diced
Fresh thyme
1 clove garlic, crushed
Juice of 1 lemon
1 bay leaf
Hollandaise sauce (see page 32)

Wash and dry the hake cutlets. Salt and pepper both sides. Set oven to gas mark 6/400°F/200°C.

Melt a little butter and gently fry the onion until translucent. Place the cutlets on the bed of onion in an ovenproof dish. Add the fresh thyme, garlic, lemon juice, bay leaf and the remainder of the butter. Cover with a buttered paper or aluminium foil and cook for about 20 minutes.

Remove the skin from the fish and place on a serving dish. Use a sieve to strain the juices from the oven dish over the fish and finally coat the cutlets with hollandaise sauce. A frond of fresh fennel on each cutlet would be a perfect garnish.

Sonia and I once swigged down quite a lot of English white wine whilst eating this dish. We felt no particular pain as a result!

Japanese Sashimi and Tempura; *Over*: Marinated Fish with Yoghurt and Spices

J

A JAPANESE FEAST

Despite similar ingredients, Chinese and Japanese cooking are very different. In Japan, ingredients are seldom mixed in the cooking process and, although served with many variations, great emphasis is placed on retaining the individual taste of each food.

Japanese food is exquisitely presented. Fresh flowers are used as edible garnish and delicate porcelain and lacquered wooden plates and dishes help to heighten the visual effect, resulting in the only food in the world that is allowed to break my 'use only white plates' rule. So before you start to cook, take a trip to your nearest oriental food market and obtain the right equipment: porcelain bowls, handleless cups, chopsticks, chopstick rests, lacquered serving trays, etc. Spend as much as you can afford, so that when you go Japanese for an evening you can really immerse yourself in the intrinsic feel of the meal – borrow the kids' *Sunday Times* Offer beanbags to sit on around the wicker and glass-topped table that you normally use to display your socio-literary credentials. While at the market, buy a crate of sake, which you will serve warm throughout the meal. Also some green tea – remember to buy a delicate teapot.

Japanese food is cut finely and delicately so you will need some very sharp knives. To make the slicing easier, remember to have your fish or meat well chilled. All the recipes in this book demand fresh fish, but none more so than these.

So, my little oriental gastronauts, all the wondrous flavours of the East can be yours if you follow my instructions. (Actually it was my friend Chikako, of Chikako's Japanese Restaurant in Bath, who revealed all to me.) Each of the following recipes would make a delightful supper, but why not splash out and serve them one after the other at a highly sophisticated dinner party for nine or ten of your closest friends?

Sliced Raw Fish (Sashimi)

Now here is a dish to impress with. A culinary testament to your aesthetic taste and flair for stunning visual effects. You might even greet your guests with the phrase *konichi wah* and mutter other Japanese phrases to your spouse or lover out of clear earshot. During the meal, apologise once or twice for not having any *mirin* or *napa*, but do not of course explain what they are. You do this by looking at your loved one and saying, 'Pity we couldn't get any *kombu*. Mr Koo is so unreliable these days.' Then arch your eyebrows in a marked manner before continuing, 'I adore *sashimi*, it has such *shibui*.'*

* Economy of elegance

Serves 4–5

1 ½ lb (750 g) skinless fillets of *fresh, fresh* bass, salmon, scallops and mackerel
8 oz (225 g) large prawns, unshelled
6 oz (175 g) white radish (*daikon*), shredded
1 carrot, shredded into long thin strands
4–5 spring onions, cut lengthways
1 tablespoon green horseradish powder (another visit to the oriental market)
1 tablespoon grated fresh ginger
Lemon wedges
Japanese soy sauce (*shoyu*)

Slice the fish into very thin rounds, except for the salmon which you cut into diamond shapes. Arrange the scallop slices, like the petals of a flower, around a serving dish. Make three peaked mountains of each of the vegetables on the same dish and lap the slices of bass and mackerel around the bases of two of them. Prop the prawns around the third, and arrange the salmon pieces to balance the display.

Mix the horseradish with a little water to make a thick paste (*wasabi*) and place on a dish with the ginger and lemon wedges. Pour the soy sauce into individual bowls and allow each guest to add ginger and *wasabi* to taste. The fish is then dipped into this mixture and eaten. Tepid plain boiled rice can be served with it.

Japanese Fritters (Tempura)

These delicate fritters are a delight, visually and gastronomically pleasing. You can use all sorts of ingredients – thin batons of fish or vegetables, fried in a light vegetable oil in a fondue-set at the table. Make the batter immediately prior to cooking and it must be cold.

Serves 4– 5

1 lb (450 g) large prawns, peeled with the tails still on
12 mange-touts or snow peas
2 courgettes, cut into 2 in (5 cm) batons
10 mushrooms, finely sliced
1 onion, finely sliced
Bland oil for deep frying

For the batter:
2 oz (50 g) flour
2 oz (50 g) cornflour
1 teaspoon baking powder
½ teaspoon salt
1 egg, beaten
7 fl oz (200 ml) iced water
1 ice cube

For the dipping sauce:

½ pint (300 ml) Japanese stock/*dashi* (see page 29), or buy a packet from an oriental market

2 tablespoons Japanese soy sauce (*shoyu*)

3 tablespoons sweet rice wine or dry sherry mixed with sugar – do not use a sweet sherry

Pinch salt

For the garnish:

3 tablespoons grated fresh ginger

2 tablespoons shredded carrot

4 tablespoons puréed white radish (*daikon*)

Petals of 4 marigolds

To make the batter, put all the dry ingredients into a cold mixing bowl. Mix the water and egg together and add to the bowl, whisking gently. Keep cool with the ice cube.

For the dipping sauce, mix all the ingredients together, bring to the boil and keep hot. Heat the oil to 350°F/180°C – drop in a cube of bread: if it turns quickly golden the temperature is right, if it burns or just sits there, adjust the heat accordingly. Dip the prawns and vegetables into the batter and fry a few at a time. Shake them free of oil and place on a central serving dish, strewn with marigold petals. The hot sauce is already in individual dishes in front of your guests, into which they will stir ginger, carrot and radish to taste, to make an excellent dip for these crispy little dreams.

Teppanyaki

Teppan means iron, *yaki* to fry. So before you can begin you will need an electric griddle (not less than 18 × 20 in/46 × 50 cm) to pop on the table so each guest can cook his own bits.

Any combination of fish, fowl, meat or vegetables can be used. As usual with Japanese cooking, the meat or fish should be cut into mouth-size pieces, the vegetables into thin strips or slices.

Serves 4

9 oz (250 g) sirloin or fillet steak, cut into cubes

8 large prawns, unshelled

1 chicken breast, skinned, boned and cubed

9 oz (250 g) fillet of cod, cubed

4 spring onions, shredded

9 oz (250 g) fresh beansprouts

16 scallops

5 oz (150 g) button mushrooms, sliced

4 small courgettes, cut into thin rounds

Vegetable oil

For the bitter sauce (*ponzu*):

4 fl oz (110 ml) Japanese soy sauce (*shoyu*)

4 fl oz (110 ml) lemon juice

4 tablespoons sweet rice wine or dry sherry mixed with sugar – do not use sweet sherry

For the mustard sauce (*karashi jyoyu*):

2 teaspoons dry mustard

2 teaspoons hot water

3 tablespoons Japanese soy sauce (*shoyu*)

2 tablespoons rice wine vinegar (*su*), or add sugar and water to white wine vinegar

1 teaspoon nut oil

Make the bitter sauce by mixing all the ingredients together and pouring into individual dishes. Make the mustard sauce by mixing the dry mustard with the water. Stir in the other ingredients and serve in individual bowls.

Arrange the uncooked food decoratively on a dish. Heat the electric griddle and brush lightly with oil. Cook the pieces of fish, meat and vegetables on both sides for a minute or two and dip into the sauces.

L

LANGOUSTINES (DUBLIN BAY PRAWNS)

What a cruel trick to take the delicate flesh of these fine prawns, cover them in E76, vegetable oil, emulsifying salts, artificial breadcrumbs, freeze them and call them scampi. A super way to cook fresh ones is simply to poach them in a court bouillon (see page 29) and serve with mayonnaise or *aioli* (see pages 32 & 30). They also grill well on the barbecue.

Langoustines Vauclusienne

Serves 4

5 tablespoons olive oil

1 carrot, finely chopped

1 onion, finely chopped

48 langoustines

1 fl oz (25 ml) Cognac or *eau de vie*

4 fl oz (110 ml) dry white wine

¾ pint (400 ml) fresh tomato sauce (see page 34)

¼ teaspoon *harissa* or chilli sauce

1 clove garlic, partly crushed

1 bouquet garni

Heat the olive oil in a large pan and add the carrot, onion and prawns. Cook briskly for 3 minutes. Add the Cognac, flame the dish and then add the white wine and cook for a further 2 minutes.

Add the tomato sauce, chilli sauce, garlic and bouquet garni and simmer for 4 or 5 minutes more. Take care not to overcook. You must adjust the cooking times according to the size of the prawns.

LOBSTER (OR CRAYFISH/CRAWFISH)

If you want elaborate dishes of lobster or crayfish, cut into petals and garnished with roe soufflés and barques of filo pastry delicately stuffed with morilles and truffles in a light pink sauce made from sea urchins, I suggest that you hot-foot it to one of the better three-star Michelin restaurants across the Channel, because your fish correspondent, sick to the back teeth of British-style frozen/cooked lobster thermidor (or whatever floury rose-coloured sauce and cheese they pour over it), says that there is only one way to cook a lobster. Even in France, in restaurants charging £35 per kilo for a cooked lobster, they are microwaving precooked, frozen, conditioned crustaceans and presenting them as freshly boiled!

It would be a disaster to spend the fortune necessary to cook lobsters my way for friends who may not appreciate that this method has real *shibui* (see Japanese recipes, page 69), so why not experiment on yourself first?

The crayfish is tougher than the lobster, but I think has the finer flavour.

NB A preboiled lobster, reheated under the grill with butter, is not a grilled lobster.

Grilled Lobster

1 live lobster, approx 1 ½ lb (700 g)
4 oz (110 g) best unsalted butter
Juice of 1 lemon
Pinch fine sea salt and a twist or two of black pepper
1 bottle Château Grillet 1970 or 1976

With a sharp 12 in (30.5 cm) cook's knife, kill the lobster with a sharp plunge through the back of the head. Then cut it in half lengthways. Remove the black or greenish sac from the head and the black or green thread which runs the length of the body.

Preheat the grill. Place the lobster on a grilling tray, season with salt, pepper and little knobs of butter and cook under the hot grill for 10–15 minutes, or until the shell on the claws has turned pink.

Upon your finest polished table, set with crystal and silver, there will be silver jugs of melted butter and lemon juice. Before eating, check that the petals have not fallen from the red roses that add the only colour to the otherwise cool and sombre room. If the telephone rings, ignore it. A smile of satisfaction is quite in order as you pour the pale-green Château Grillet into a large glass, and sip in silent splendour as you contemplate the milky flesh of your lobster.

Eating alone has its compensations.

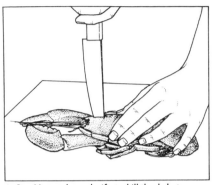
▲ 1   Use a sharp knife to kill the lobster

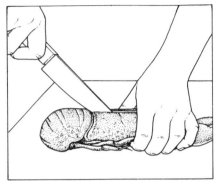
▲ 2   Cut in half lengthways

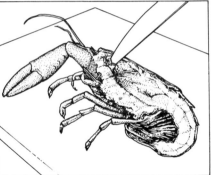
▲ 3   Remove the black or green thread

M

MARINATED FISH

Although men are supposed to be showing more interest in cooking than ever before, it is still the ladies who do most of it at home. As much as you may like the idea of getting the old man to prepare the supper, you probably can't face the resulting mess in the kitchen – of course he will have been 'too busy creating' to clear up – not to mention the risk of him wrecking expensive ingredients which will leave you either hungry or ill. But if you start him off on something that he can't ruin, which is stylish, novel and, most importantly, enables him to have a few slurps on the side, you may gradually turn him into a more useful human being.

Persuade him to prepare the cold lunch for next Sunday's summer snack (by hinting that iced schnapps, cold lager and a simple potato salad are the right accompaniments for three contrasting dishes of marinated herring, salmon and mackerel). The essential thing is to be out of the house on the fateful day that he makes his first tentative steps into the kitchen. Otherwise he will just stand there reading the recipe and drinking the schnapps and you will whizz around doing all the work. So arrange with a friend to call you with a phoney emergency just as he starts. If he is successful with these dishes you may allow him later to graduate to *sashimi* (see page 69) with, of course, the inevitable reward of sake. And before you know where you are, he will be boring the pub with his tales of culinary derring-do.

Marinated Raw Herring Fillets

Serves 4–6

12 fresh herring fillets (ask the fishmonger to prepare them)
1 tablespoon finely chopped capers
1 red onion, very finely chopped

For the marinade:
1 pint (570 ml) good white wine vinegar (nothing else will do)
1 red onion, finely sliced
2 tablespoons coarse sea salt
2 cloves
6–8 crushed black peppercorns
1 large bay leaf
1 fresh red chilli, halved
A drop or two of tabasco sauce
2 teaspoons white sugar

Lay the fillets, skin down, and spread each one with the chopped onion and capers. Roll them up and fasten with cocktail sticks to prevent them unrolling. Mix the marinade ingredients together and place the rolled herrings in it. Seal with an airtight lid and leave in the larder or fridge for at least 4 days before eating.

This recipe is British. Do not cheat by buying the fillets pre-prepared; they are just not good enough.

Gravlax

Serves 4–6

Now to Scandinavia for the marinated salmon, a simple and delicious delight:

> 2–3 lb (900 g–1.4 kg) middle-cut fresh salmon, boned and cut into two lengthways
> A handful fresh dill (i.e. lots)
> 4 tablespoons coarse sea salt
> 2 tablespoons caster sugar
> 2 tablespoons crushed black peppercorns

Lay one fillet, skin down, in a non-metal dish. Cover with the dill, salt, sugar and black pepper. Lay the remaining salmon fillet, skin up, on top.

Find a piece of hardboard a little larger than the fish, cover it with aluminium-foil and place it, well weighted, on the fish. Stand in the fridge for at least 72 hours. Turn it every 12 hours; every time you turn it, spoon the juices that have oozed out over the fish as if you were basting a turkey.

Ceviche

Serves 4–6

Lastly to Mexico for the quickest recipe:

> 6 fillets of mackerel, cut lengthways in half so that you have 12 thin pieces (bass would
> be an excellent alternative)

> **For the marinade:**
> Juice of 3–4 limes
> 1 fresh red chilli, finely chopped
> 1 red onion, very thinly sliced
> Sea salt and ground black pepper to taste
> 1 clove garlic, finely chopped

Lay the fillets side by side, but not overlapping, in a shallow dish. Pour over the marinade and leave for 3 or 4 hours in the fridge. Turn the fillets at least 3 times during this period.

And there you have it: if you prepare all three of the above recipes you could invite at least 10 people for a multinational fish feast.

MARINATED FISH WITH YOGHURT AND SPICES

The wise man dismisses nothing.
He stands at the banks of a fast-flowing river.
Not dismayed by the raging torrent that blocks his path.
He wonders where it is going.
And while pondering upon these thoughts, he will sip a glass of
lassi.
This iced and salted yoghurt, flavoured with aromatics, will free his
mind of concern and liberate the gastric juices and turn his thoughts

to the fragrant spices of the orient. Which, my friends, can be yours if you follow these instructions:

Serves 6

> 6 trout
> ½ teaspoon paprika
> 4 tablespoons coriander seeds
> ½ teaspoon salt
> 6 cardomom seeds
> 2 onions, finely chopped
> 2 cloves garlic
> ¼ teaspoon ground black pepper
> 1 tablespoon dill
> ½ green pepper, deseeded
> 2 tablespoons freshly chopped mint
> Juice of 1 lemon
> 6 oz (175 ml) natural yoghurt
> Butter for basting

Instead of trout, you can use whiting or perch, or thick fillets of white fish such as hake or cod.

Place all the other ingredients, except the yoghurt, in your liquidiser (or pestle and mortar). Whizz or grind until you have a paste which you then mix with the natural yoghurt.

Clean the fish and spread the paste over and inside them. Leave to marinate for 1 hour.

Grill over a wood fire or under a preheated grill until crisp and cooked. During the cooking process, you should turn the fish from time to time, and baste with butter and the remainder of the marinade.

As you sip your iced lager and flake the flesh of the fish into freshly baked *nan* bread, uplifted with a fine lime pickle, you may wonder what the first sentences of this recipe signify.

But, as they say in the East, if you have to ask you will never know.

MONGOLIAN FISH HOTPOT

This is not only a gastronomic treat of the utmost delicacy but also a visual delight, and although you can use your cast-iron fondue set to boil the stock in which you cook at the table, it would be much better to buy the correct Mongolian Fire or Chafing Pot. It comes with little wire baskets with which you can fish out your merry morsels. You also need small bowls for the sauces, which are placed before each guest so that they can mix them to their taste, bowls to eat from and chopsticks to eat with. And because at the end of the banquet you should drink the liquid in which the fish has been cooked, you will also need china spoons.

All the specialist ingredients for the Mongolian Fish Hotpot can be obtained from a Chinese supermarket.

Serves 6–8

3 lb (1.4 kg) of the freshest raw fish, perhaps a mixture of:
Fresh scallops, cut in half sideways
Thin slivers of squid
Whole large prawns, peeled with heads and tails on
Thin fillets skinned lemon or Dover sole
Fork-sized cubes of salmon
1 lb (450 g) young spinach leaves
8 oz (225 g) broccoli spears, with thin trimmed stalks
2 lb (900 g) Chinese cabbage, cut into pieces
12 slices bean curd cake
4 oz (110 g) transparent noodles, soaked in water for 10 minutes and drained

For the dips:
Hoi sin sauce
Chilli sauce
2 parts soy sauce mixed with 1 part sesame seed oil
4 parts finely chopped spring onion mixed with 1 part finely chopped ginger and garlic

To serve:
4 pints (2.3 litres) water
2 chicken stock cubes

To serve, bring the water to the boil. Dissolve the stock cubes in it. Using their little nets guests can alternately dip fish, vegetables, noodles and bean curd cake into the bubbling liquid for 20 or 30 seconds and then dip into one of the four dips as they choose.

When all the fish has gone, add the remaining vegetables to the boiling pot, and if necessary more water, and serve as soup.

MONKFISH

From being despised as false scampi a few years ago, monkfish has shot from obscurity and now features on menus across the country in a green peppercorn sauce, which is just as unfair since, to my mind, as it is generally indifferently cooked, it turns out to be a pretty grim dish. This is a fish that does not lend itself easily to cream sauces (with the notable exception of the following recipe).

Floyd's Monkfish (conceived and first executed on board a trawler off the south-west coast of England)

Serves 2

> 1 oz (25 g) butter
> 4 thin fillets monkfish
> 2 rashers smoked bacon, diced
> 1 shallot, chopped
> 1 clove garlic, crushed
> Juice of 1 lemon
> 1 bay leaf
> 1 sprig fresh thyme
> A little parsley, chopped
> Salt and pepper
> ¼ pint (150 ml) double cream
> 1 egg yolk
> 1 glass dry white wine
> 1 fishing trawler and crew

Melt the butter in a pan and gently fry the fish for a minute. Add everything else, except the wine, egg yolk and cream, and cook for about 10 minutes. Add the wine and remove the fish to a warm plate. Bubble up the sauce for 1 minute and then stir in the cream, reduce the heat and briskly whisk in the egg yolk. Pour the sauce over the monkfish and serve.

Roast Monkfish with Garlic

Serves 4

> Tail of monkfish, about 2¼ lb (generous kg)
> 1 bulb plump garlic, fresh as possible
> ½ fl oz (15 ml) olive oil
> ¼ teaspoon fresh thyme leaves
> ¼ teaspoon fennel seeds
> Juice of 1 lemon
> Salt and pepper
> 1 bay leaf
> Tomatoes to accompany

Set the oven to gas mark 7/425°F/220°C. Skin the fish carefully, leaving no trace of the thin membrane under the skin, and remove the central bone. Wash and dry it and finally tie it up with string like a piece of meat.

Peel 2 cloves of garlic and cut into thin slices. Make some incisions in the fish and push in the garlic slices.

In a frying pan, heat the olive oil and brown the fish on all sides for about 5 minutes. Season with salt, pepper, thyme, fennel and lemon juice and pop into a baking tray along with a tablespoon of olive oil. Arrange the remainder of the unpeeled garlic bulb around the dish, pop the bay leaf under the fish and cook in the oven for about 20 minutes.

Grilled tomatoes should accompany this dish. Encourage your guests to overcome their reticence and eat the roasted garlic

Monkfish and Salmon Terrine

Serves 4

1 oz (25 g) butter
1 lb (450 g) whole fresh spinach leaves, blanched and drained
12 oz (350 g) fillet of monkfish (or bass or good white fish such as sole or turbot)
2 fl oz (50 ml) double cream
1 whole egg
1 egg white
1 tablespoon lemon juice
Salt and pepper
Large pinch cayenne pepper
4 oz (110 g) fillet fresh salmon, without skin or bones
Rémoulade sauce (see page 34)

Butter a deep-sided terrine mould and lay leaves of spinach over the inside, allowing folds to hang over the outside so that the terrine can be completely wrapped in spinach. Set the oven to gas mark 6/400°F/200°C.

Process the monkfish in the liquidiser for 2 or 3 minutes. Add the cream, eggs, lemon juice, a pinch of salt, 7 twists of pepper and the cayenne, and whizz for a further 2 minutes.

Fill half of the terrine with this mixture and cover it with thin slices of salmon. Cover with the remaining mixture and fold over the spinach leaves.

Cover the terrine with aluminium foil and bake in a bain-marie for about 40 minutes. Allow to cool overnight and tip out on to a serving dish. When sliced, the terrine will be layered in green, white and pink. Serve with a crisp salad, dressed with walnut oil and pine-nuts, and a rémoulade sauce.

MOUSSES

Hot fish mousses make excellent starters or light lunches and if you have a liquidiser they are easy to prepare. You can use practically any fish you like. Nadine Perrigault of Restaurant L'Armada in Cancale, Brittany, showed me a delightful dish of artichokes stuffed with red mullet mousse, garnished with hollandaise sauce, which made a superb lunch. Equally, trout, perch or any white fish adapt well to mousses but, unlike the stronger-flavoured red mullet, will need a more powerful sauce, such as shellfish sauce. I do not recommend smoked fish for these dishes.

Artichokes Stuffed with Red Mullet Mousse and Hollandaise Sauce (From the Restaurant L'Armada, Cancale, France)

Serves 4

4 globe artichokes
10 oz (275 g) fillet of red mullet, skinned
Salt and pepper
Scant pint (½ litre) double cream
2 egg whites, beaten
4 fresh scallops
Hollandaise sauce (see page 32)

Remove the stalk from each artichoke. Then, with a very sharp knife, cut off the top of the artichoke, about two-thirds from the base. Discard the tops.

Boil the artichokes in salted water until tender (when the outer leaves can be easily detached) – about 40 minutes. Strain and leave to cool. Hold the artichoke carefully, so that the big leaves do not fall off and, with your forefinger and thumb, remove the insides, which are very little leaves and a thistly substance (the choke). Throw this away.

Make the mousse by seasoning the mullet with salt and pepper and purée in the liquidiser. Pour in the cream and whizz for a few seconds more. Chill this mixture for 5 minutes or so in the deep freeze, and then fold in the beaten egg white.

Set the oven to gas mark 5/375°F/190°C. Stuff the artichokes with the mousse and 1 scallop each. Place in a tray of water (the water must not touch the mousse) and bake in the oven for about 30 minutes. Strain carefully from the water and mask with hollandaise sauce.

To make individual mousses, of let us say trout, this is what you need.

Trout Mousse

Serves 4

1¼ lb (550 g) trout, boned and skinned
3–4 tablespoons salt
3–4 teaspoons fresh black pepper
1¾ pints (1 litre) double cream
4 egg whites, well beaten

Season the trout with salt and pepper and purée in the liquidiser. Pour in the cream and whizz for a few seconds more. Chill this mixture for 5 minutes or so in the deep freeze, and then fold in the beaten egg whites.

Set the oven to gas mark 5/375°F/190°C. Butter individual dishes and fill with the trout mixture. Place the dishes into a baking tray half-filled with water and cook in the oven for about 45 minutes. Garnish with crayfish sauce, shrimp butter or even anchovy butter (see pages 31, 28), depending on your taste and financial resources.

MUSSELS

Mussels are plentiful, cheap and delicious but not really rated by the great British gastronaut, who seems to prefer frozen prawns in tomato-flavoured salad cream to shellfish in general and mussels in particular.

Mussels are best in the winter months. (Our French neighbours make no such seasonal distinction.) Many prefer the tiny Dutch or French mussels, some the huge Spanish ones (often eaten raw by the natives), but my favourite is the plump, orange-fleshed, English mussel.

I once had a feast of mussels, cockles, whelks and oysters, all the best that I have ever eaten, at Len Hodge's oyster farm at Frenchman's Creek in Cornwall. I sat in his garden, overlooking the Helford river, on one of those classic burnt autumnal days, gorging myself on the fruit of his farm, oblivious to a light but persistent drizzle, enjoying myself enormously, while Len spun yarns of Cornish myths and epicurean feasts of days gone by.

The bore of mussels is cleaning them. For vast quantities in my restaurant, we would spin them in a washing machine, but however you do it, you must observe the following rules:

1   Wash thoroughly under cold running water.
2   Scrape each one free of barnacles and seaweed, until they sparkle like black pearls.
3   Rip off the fibrous beard which protrudes between the shells.
4   Push each mussel sideways – if it won't budge it is not full of sand, so go ahead and use it. If it does, discard it.
5   Do not use any cracked or open mussels. If some mussels are open, pump them for a second or two between forefinger and thumb, if they close again they are still OK.
6   Rinse again under cold water.

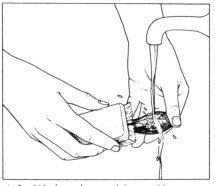

▲ 1   Wash each mussel thoroughly

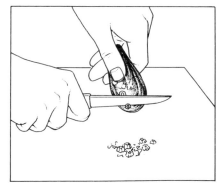

▲ 2   Scrape off the barnacles

▲ 3 Pull away the beard

Mussels in White Wine

Serves 4–6

6 lb (2.8 kg) mussels
2 oz (50 g) butter
2 large onions, chopped
3 cloves garlic, chopped
¼ pint (300 ml) dry white wine
2 tablespoons chopped parsley (1 for cooking, 1 for garnish)
Salt and pepper

Clean the mussels. Melt the butter in a large pan. Add the onion and garlic and cook for 2 or 3 minutes. Add the wine and bring to the boil. Add the other ingredients, cover with a lid, and boil, shaking the pan from time to time, until the mussels steam open.

Serve with more knobs of butter and parsley strewn over. Use plenty of bread to mop up the sauce.

Gratin of Mussels with Spinach

Serves 4

50 mussels, i.e. 4–5 pints (2.3–2.8 litres) depending on size
1¼ lb (550 g) fresh young spinach
¼ pint (150 ml) béchamel sauce (see page 31)
2 fl oz (50 ml) double cream beaten with yolk of 1 egg
1½ oz (40 g) Gruyère cheese, grated
Salt and pepper

Clean the mussels, and steam them open in a lidded pan with one cup of water, for 2 or 3 minutes. Save the resulting juice and remove the mussels from their shells. Discard the shells.

Wash the spinach and shake it fairly dry. Pop into a saucepan over a low heat. Do not add any water but cook gently just in the water that

83

has been retained on the leaves after washing, until you can mash the spinach easily. Strain off all excess liquid.

Mix the mussels, spinach and béchamel sauce together in an ovenproof dish. Stir in 2 tablespoons of the juice from the mussels and the egg and cream mixture. Mix well, season and sprinkle with the grated Gruyère. Brown in a hot oven for 10 minutes or so.

Mussel Risotto

Serves 4

> 3 tablespoons olive oil
> 1 onion, chopped
> 1 leek, chopped
> 1 large ripe tomato, peeled and chopped
> 9 oz (250 g) arborio (Italian) rice
> 1 glass dry white wine
> 18 fl oz (500 ml) water
> 24 mussels (or clams), immaculately cleaned
> 2 cloves garlic, crushed
> 1 bouquet garni
> Sachet of saffron
> Salt and pepper

Put the olive oil in a large frying pan (or *paella*) over a low heat and sauté the onion, leek and tomato for 2 or 3 minutes or until the onion begins to colour.

Add the rice and mix thoroughly with the oil and vegetables until every grain is coated with oil. Add the wine and stir constantly until all the wine has been absorbed.

Add the water and mussels, garlic, bouquet garni, saffron and salt and pepper. Cover the dish with a lid and cook slowly for about 20 minutes or until the rice has absorbed the liquid. Don't keep lifting the lid to see how the rice is getting on; it won't burn or stick too much if you have followed this recipe to the letter.

Roast Monkfish with Garlic; *Over*: Artichoke Stuffed with Red Mullet Mousse

O

OYSTERS

Ah, the oyster. The crazy oyster.

These androgynous aphrodisiacs, once the staple diet of poor apprentices, are now the currency of credibility for the Gucci-shoed executive who also swallows big deals as he sips a glass of Chablis in the dim blue-suited bars of the capital.

To alight at Paddington from the West and take a taxi to Swallow Street for a dozen at Bentley's at 11.00 am is one of the great pleasures left to the provincial, before tackling the tasks of the metropolis and a later lunch. White-coated waiters with a military air fix you with unseeing eyes and deftly flop off the shells with the precision of a Guardsman on parade, clacking the white plate of No. Ones on the zinc before you.

The Portuguese oyster is gaining popularity, but for me cannot compare with the Colchesters or Whitstables, or especially the plump and sweet oyster from the Helford river. But the *very* best that I have ever had were at the George Hotel at Bridport, when I ate 40 beauties from Poole to celebrate my birthday.

It is unthinkable to cook oysters, but Americans do: Oysters Rockefeller, raped, to my mind, with a stuffing of spinach, cream and Pernod, are supposed to be great. Even a culinary giant such as Paul Bocuse proposes that we should grill oysters with breadcrumbs and herbs. But no. No. A good oyster needs only a hint of lemon juice, good company and a hearty appetite. For fun.

P

PAELLA

There is nothing like a yellow mountain of paella after a hard day wind-surfing or lolling on the beach, glass in hand, under a merciless sun, and since it is really a one-pot dish, it makes an ideal holiday or party supper.

It is very important to follow the cooking instructions carefully. Don't cheat by precooking the rice and then stirring in precooked prawns and chicken. You may, of course, vary the ingredients to suit availability or taste. But remember, ingredients serve only to enhance the rice, not the reverse. And it is all right if the rice sticks to the bottom of the pan and burns a little. Bags I scrape out the dish. . . .

An Authentic Paella

Serves 6

2 fl oz (50 ml) olive oil
1 ¼ lb (550 g) rabbit pieces or chicken pieces, diced
Salt and pepper
1 large onion, chopped
1 red pepper, with pith and seeds removed and cut into 2 in (5 cm) squares or thin strips
4 cloves garlic, chopped
12 oz (350 g) good rice, well washed and dried
25 fl oz (750 ml) water
1 teaspoon fresh rosemary and thyme leaves
2 sachets of saffron
50 mussels, cleaned
24 clams, if available
1 small octopus or squid, cleaned and chopped
12 langoustines (Dublin Bay prawns)
2 tablespoons pine-nuts

Heat the olive oil in a large iron sauté pan (you should really have a *paella*) and fry the seasoned rabbit or chicken for 3 or 4 minutes. Add the chopped onion, red pepper and garlic and fry with the meat until golden.

Add the rice and stir well until every grain is well coated with oil and thoroughly mixed with the other ingredients – if necessary, add a little more olive oil. Add the water, the fresh herbs, saffron, clams, mussels and squid; cover with a large lid and cook gently for 20 minutes.

Remove the lid and add the langoustines and cook for a further 10 minutes. Finally sprinkle in the pine-nuts and serve.

As long as you have used a heavy iron pan and cook over a low heat your paella should not burn or stick – although a slightly caramelised base is actually the ideal if you can achieve it. Do not be tempted to lift the lid every 5 seconds to see how it is going; you will only slow down the cooking process and end up with hard rice and overcooked fish.

PERCH

Perch is a freshwater bass with fine, closely grained flesh, sweet and delicious. As a lad, I often cooked them over a twig fire on cold winter mornings whilst fishing. If you get any perch, take care of the spines on the fin, which are quite unpleasant.

There is a street of restaurants in Lyons where every menu features perch. Deep fried in a light batter is a simple and good way, or baked in a paper envelope, but the dish that I enjoyed best was this one:

Perch Fillets with Sage

Serves 4

> 8 fillets of perch
> 1/2 pint (300 ml) double cream
> 1 1/2 oz (40 g) butter
> 10 fresh sage leaves
> Salt and pepper

Wash and dry the perch and set the oven to gas mark 7/425°F/220°C.

Put the cream into a saucepan and bring to the boil. Butter a baking tray with half of the butter. Put in the sage and lay the fillets on top. Add salt and pepper and cover with the warm cream. Scatter the remaining butter in lumps over the cream. Bake in the oven for about 15 minutes.

PIKE

You may be forced to catch your own pike before you can enjoy the fine flavour of this 'freshwater shark' (though I know that Vin Sullivan in Abergavenny can always get you one). Years ago it was a popular eating fish in this country, especially with the monks who feasted on freshwater fish, often farmed, when they 'fasted' on Fridays. Merrily they took their places at the long refectory tables which groaned with pewter platters piled high with braised carp, fried perch, steamed tench, stewed eels and baked pike. In France, of course, pike is easily available and recipes for it appear as a matter of course in cookery books. In the Loire valley it is hard to escape from *Quennelles de Brochet*, a sausage-shaped steamed fish dumpling.

I caught my first sizeable pike in March 1985 on the River Tone one morning, near Taunton, as a thin mist hung over the Somerset Flats and a pale sun glinted on the sluggish river, like a ribbon of lead, as it ran through the stunted willows. And to celebrate I created this recipe:

Pike with Red Pepper Sauce

Serves 4

> 4 fillets of pike, skinned
> 1 medium red pepper, depithed, seeded and cut into 4
> 1 teaspoon tomato purée
> 2 glasses dry white wine
> 1 pint (570 ml) water
> 1 bay leaf
> 1 crushed clove garlic
> 1 teaspoon chopped parsley
> 1/2 onion, finely chopped
> 4 tablespoons double cream
> 2 egg yolks
> Salt and pepper

Boil the red pepper and purée it. Add the tomato purée and set aside.

Mix the wine with the water, add the bay leaf, garlic, parsley, onion and a pinch of salt. Pour over the pike fillets and simmer gently for 10 to 15 minutes till the fillets are cooked. Remove the fillets to a serving dish and keep warm.

Take ⅓ of the poaching liquid, including the onion etc, and transfer to a small saucepan. Add the red pepper and tomato purée and simmer to reduce by a quarter.

When reduced, stir in the cream, whisking the while. When well mixed tip in the egg yolks and whisk furiously over a low heat until the sauce thickens. Season with salt and pepper. Strain this light pink sauce through a fine sieve over the pike fillets and serve.

PILCHARDS

Pilchards are a large sardine and whatever you can do to a sardine, you can do to a pilchard. That is charcoal grill them, can them in olive oil or tomato sauce, or bake them gently in vinegar, onions and cloves. Jolly nice too. Especially the tinned ones in tomato sauce on toast.

Charcoal Grilled Pilchards

This simple dish can be prepared with ease in the evening calm of your summer garden for a few unexpected guests at a very modest price.

Serves 4

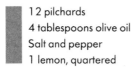

12 pilchards
4 tablespoons olive oil
Salt and pepper
1 lemon, quartered

Clean and gut the pilchards. Season with salt and pepper and brush with olive oil. Grill lightly for 5 minutes on each side. Squeeze the lemon juice over and savagely eat the fish with your fingers.

Escabeche

Once a year, in the village in which I lived and worked in France, a horse-racing festival was held. In the blazing heat of July the entire village would turn out to picnic and gamble in the verdant, tree-sheltered oasis of the racetrack. My mate, known as 'Marseilles Pete', used to bring along some cold fish in a piquant tomato sauce, which was called *escabeche*. We ate it, after the cold truffle omelette that I had brought, with fresh bread and countless litres of dry rosé.

Serves 4 as a starter or 2 as a main dish

1 1/4 lb (550 g) pilchard fillets (you could use herring fillets, too)
A little milk
Flour for dredging
1/2 pint (300 ml) olive oil
1 carrot, diced
1 onion, diced
3 cloves garlic, crushed
3 tablespoons tomato purée
1/4 teaspoon cayenne pepper
1/4 pint (150 ml) white wine vinegar
1 bay leaf
Sprig fresh thyme and parsley, chopped
Salt and pepper

Dip the fillets in milk and dredge in flour. Fry in hot olive oil for 2 minutes on each side. Transfer the fish to an earthenware dish.

Take all the other ingredients and simmer until cooked – about 20 minutes. Pour this sauce over the fillets and serve chilled.

R

RED MULLET

In Spain and around the Mediterranean generally, small red mullet are grilled with their intestines and considered a great delicacy. In France they tend to remove the guts but leave the liver, which is highly prized. As a general rule, red mullet are fried or grilled. They do not lend themselves to poaching. As with grey mullet, the red mullet must be carefully scaled. Red mullet imported from around India are not so good as the Mediterranean or British ones. If you are planning to barbecue them, leave the scales on and the liver inside and brush the fish inside and out with herb oil (see page 29).

Red Mullet in Envelopes

Serves 4

8 red mullet, about 6 oz (175 g) each
4 sprigs fresh fennel fronds, or fresh basil or rosemary
2 tablespoons olive oil
Salt and pepper
Greaseproof paper or foil
Anchovy butter (see page 28)

Wash, scale, gut (leaving the liver in) and dry the mullet and pop some fresh herbs into each one. Set the oven to gas mark 7/425°F/220°C.

Cut the greaseproof paper into rectangles large enough to envelop each fish. Oil each fish and place it in the centre of the paper. Add another sprig of herbs, salt and pepper and close the envelopes. Pop these fishy letters into the oven for about 12 minutes and serve with anchovy butter.

S

SALMON

There is no point in using frozen salmon. If you can't buy a fresh one, don't bother. Better a few fillets of fresh cod with anchovy butter or a good old-fashioned tinned salmon sandwich with cucumber and vinegar.

I must say I am extremely fond of cold, poached salmon with mayonnaise and cucumber, preferably cooked and served by somebody else under the shade of elegant trees on a manicured lawn. In your crumpled lightweight suit and with a bottle of Meursault at hand there is no better way of posing in the English summer. It is best to avoid any sporting context when indulging in the art of cold salmon eating. Rowing boats and galloping horses are a distraction at a time when you need all your energy to look languidly interesting to the blonde in white silk currently talking to a guy in grey shoes.

Cold Salmon

Serves 8 as a feast, or 16 as a lunch dish

> 1 salmon, about 10 lb (4.5 kg), cleaned and gutted
> Approximately 8 pints (4.5 litres) court bouillon (see page 29)
> 1 ½ pints (700 ml) mayonnaise (see page 32)
> 2 cucumbers, peeled, cut in half lengthways, depipped and sliced thinly in crescent
>   shapes (to represent fish scales)

Put the salmon into a fish kettle and cover with the cold bouillon. Bring to the boil and leave to cook for 10 minutes. Turn off the heat and leave to cool with the lid on the fish kettle.

Remove the cold salmon carefully to a clear space and remove the bones and skin from the body – leave the skin on the head. Arrange on a suitably grand dish and coat the salmon with mayonnaise. Lay the cucumber slivers over the mayonnaise to resemble scales.

Tie on a clean apron and walk slowly and deliberately into the garden where the staff have prepared a white-napped table to receive this centrepiece of the luncheon. Ignore the man in the grey shoes who, having failed with the blonde, will now try the cook.

Salmon in Aspic

Serves 4

9 oz (250 g) fresh salmon, without skin or bones
Salt and pepper
½ pint (300 ml) dry white wine and water, mixed
1 tablespoon finely chopped parsley mixed with finely chopped, fresh tarragon
1 hard-boiled egg, the white and yolk separated and finely chopped
2 lemons, peeled, pipped, pithed and cut into small segments of ¼ in (6 mm)
½ tablespoon green peppercorns
1½ oz (40 g) tinned red pepper, strained and diced into ¼ in (6 mm) squares
1 sachet aspic jelly
Iced tomato sauce equally mixed with mayonnaise (see pages 34 & 32)

Cut the salmon into ¾ in (1.5 cm) cubes and season with salt and pepper. Simmer in the wine and water for about 3 minutes until the cubes are lightly cooked. Allow to cool in the liquid.

Remove the salmon pieces to a terrine and gently mix in the herbs, egg pieces, lemon pieces, peppercorns and red pepper. Strain the cooking liquid through muslin, so that it is clear, and gently reheat. Add the aspic jelly (following the instructions on the sachet). Allow it to cool.

Pour the cooled liquid over the ingredients in the terrine and allow it to set in the refrigerator. To serve, slice the terrine and lay it over the iced tomato and mayonnaise sauce, which you have delicately spooned on to bright white plates.

Escalope of Salmon with Hollandaise Sauce

Serves 4

1 oz (25 g) unsalted butter
½ onion, cut into very thin strips
White of 1 leek, cut into very thin strips
1 large carrot, cut into very thin strips (julienne)
Scant pint (500 ml) strained court bouillon (see page 29) or a half-and-half mix of white wine and water
4 thin escalopes of salmon, 4 oz (110 g) each
Hollandaise sauce (see page 32)
4 puff pastry shapes, to garnish
4 fronds fresh fennel
Lemon juice
Salt and pepper

Melt the butter in a shallow pan, large enough to take the four escalopes at once, and gently fry the sliced onion, leek and carrot for 1–2 minutes. Add the bouillon and poach the fish for about 3 minutes – the escalopes must not be overcooked.

Place the fish on dinner plates and garnish each one with the sliced vegetables and moisten with 2 teaspoons of bouillon. Season well and squeeze over the lemon juice. Coat the salmon with hollandaise sauce and decorate with a pastry shape and a frond of fennel. Boiled new potatoes should be served separately.

SCALLOPS

There are two basic scallops: the great scallop, usually about 5 in (12.5 cm) in diameter and supreme for gourmandising, and the smaller but tasty queen scallop, which I like to use for less sophisticated meals, such as deep-fried scallops in batter or Chinese stir-fried scallops (see page 97).

To clean a scallop, hold the shell, hinge outwards, in a cloth and carefully slide a thin knife through the hinge (if the knife point enters deeply, ensure that it is tight against the shell on the inside, thus preventing you from cutting the scallop in half) and slide round the joint (1); twist the shell open as you slide round. Cut the scallop close to the shell (2). While rinsing under water, discard the green or black sac, leaving a scallop of pure white flesh with the pink crescent of coral (3). Some steam their scallops open in the oven, but this inevitably starts to cook them, which is not to be encouraged – although the oven method is easier.

When running my restaurant in the Vaucluse in Provence, I discovered that there exists a third type of scallop. It was brought to my attention by a sophisticated Parisian couple who walked arrogantly into my little restaurant in Rue Raspail, L'Isle-sur-la-Sorgue, and took a table. They said, in what Bertie Wooster would call a marked manner, 'You are the English man, n'est-ce pas?' I took them the menu and waited for their order. If you are not familiar with the way the French order food it goes something like this:

Man: (to wife) What will you have?
Wife: (callously) Just a steak.
Man: There is no steak.
Wife: Ooff. Then a little piece of fish. Just grilled. No salt, butter or fat.
Man: (to me) What fish have you?
I point to the menu and say 'As you see there.'
Wife: I'll have a Perrier. Very cold.
Man: How is the duck cooked?
Wife: You don't like duck.
Me: Simply roasted to order and served with its juices.

Man: I'll have the kidneys. No sauce. Or fat. It is necessary to remove the gristle in the middle. I don't like gristle. And pink. They must be pink.

Wife: I don't know. (To me) What's in the Coquille St Jacques?

Me: Just scallops, shallots, parsley, sherry, cream – thickened with an egg yolk.

Man: Yes, yes. But what is in them?

Me: Scallops.

Man: Scallops?

Me: Yes. Scallops.

Man: (the light dawning – he realises that I am a complete fool) *In France* (intoned patronisingly) Coquille St Jacques are shells stuffed with cold white fish in mayonnaise.

Not wishing to become embroiled in what would have been a futile argument, I thanked him profusely for putting me straight and prepared him and his wife this dish, which I call Scallops Rue Raspail, which she grudgingly enjoyed, obviously relieved to find no jam in it (the French think that when not smothering our meat in mint sauce we are covering it in jam). Anyway. . . .

Final score – Angleterre 29. France 0.

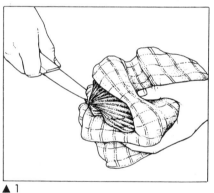
▲ 1

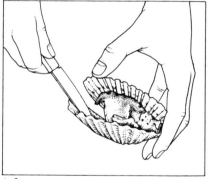
▲ 2

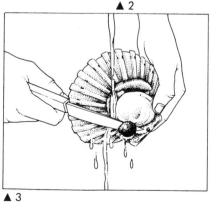
▲ 3

Scallops Rue Raspail

Serves 4

> 3½ oz (100 g) unsalted butter
> 8 fresh great scallops, cleaned and trimmed
> Salt and pepper
> 1 shallot, very finely chopped
> Half glass dry sherry
> 7 fl oz (200 ml) double cream
> 2 egg yolks, whisked
> Parsley, finely chopped

Melt the butter in a large frying pan and when it is bubbling, but *not* burning, add the scallops. Season and cook gently for 2 minutes on each side. Remove the scallops to a serving dish and keep warm. They should be slightly undercooked.

Into the juices in the pan, toss the shallot and the sherry and simmer for 5 minutes, or until you begin to worry that there might not be enough sauce. Then add the cream and, over a low heat, stir in the egg yolks until the sauce resembles a thick custard. Strain the sauce over the scallops and garnish with the chopped parsley.

NB Add the egg yolks carefully, slowly whisking all the time over a low heat, or you will end up with scrambled egg. *Doucement, doucement* is the word.

Grilled Scallops with Cointreau

Serves 4

> 16 large scallops
> 16 thin rashers of streaky bacon, with the rind off
> Sea salt and black pepper
> 1 teaspoon oregano
> Juice of 1 lemon
> 2 oz (50 g) butter
> A large measure of Cointreau
> 8 tablespoons double cream
> 1 tablespoon chopped parsley

Turn the grill to maximum heat. Wrap each scallop in bacon and thread on to 4 skewers. Season with the salt, pepper, oregano and lemon juice. Dab with nuts of butter. Put the scallops on a tray, to collect the cooking juices, and pop under the grill. As the bacon cooks, turn the skewers over. When the bacon is cooked, so are the scallops.

Place the tray of scallops, still on the skewers, over a low heat, pour over the Cointreau and flame it. Add the cream and stir into the juices. Let it bubble for a while to thicken. Serve the scallops with the sauce strained over. Garnish with parsley.

Stir-fried Scallops with Vegetables

Scallops are widely used in Chinese cooking and are ideally suited to the brisk stir-frying method, as in this recipe, which retains their juicy sweet flavour.

Serves 4

16 queen scallops, cleaned and trimmed
6 spring onions, each cut into 4 long strips
8 oz (225 g) fresh beansprouts
2 large carrots, cut into long thin julienne strips
Salt and pepper
Vegetable oil for frying
1 tablespoon dry sherry or rice wine
1/4 teaspoon grated fresh ginger
1/4 teaspoon finely chopped garlic
1 teaspoon light soy sauce
1 pinch Chinese Five-Spice powder
Juice of 1 lemon

Season the scallops with the salt and pepper and fry briskly for 2 to 3 minutes in 1 to 2 tablespoons of the oil – use a wok if you have one, otherwise a frying pan will do. Add the sherry, soy sauce, lemon juice and allow to bubble for a minute. Tip on to a dish and keep warm.

Add another tablespoon of oil to your wok. When very hot, add all the other ingredients and stir-fry over a fierce flame for 2 to 3 minutes. Return the scallops to the wok and whizz around a couple of times. Turn out on to a serving dish and serve immediately with plain steamed rice.

SEAFOOD SALADS

It is not every day that we can indulge in a feast of cold salmon or lobster salad, so I have included a few of my favourite fish salads, which you can serve either as *hors d'œuvres* or as light lunches or suppers.

Salade Niçoise

I have decided to include this wonderful rustic dish, which, properly prepared, is a great way to eat tinned fish. In recent years it has become abused as a kind of culinary kitchen sink into which any old garbage is thrown, particularly in the ubiquitous wine bars and 'theme' pubs that blight this fair island of ours. Properly prepared, with good bread and wine, it makes a marvellous starter, especially before a main meal of fish and, because most fish dishes really only need potatoes or rice, you can eliminate the howls of protest from your heathen trencherman who demands carrots, sprouts, peas and broccoli with his red mullet by pointing out that he has already had his vegetable intake by way of this great salad.

This seems a good point to emphasise that there are no kings or queens behind the gates of Château Gourmetghast. The salad lies equal with the bass or *la bourride*, the cod with the crayfish. So don't make this salad when you are pressed and stretched. Think of it as an erotic sculpture: firm, fresh, tender and well dressed! With appealing protuberances to tempt your lips, not a flabby corpse dying slowly and flat on a plate.

The quantities depend on you, but let us say this salad is going to be a main course for lunch for 4 or 5 hungry people. I am sure I will be criticised for being pedantic about a dish that varies widely in its execution throughout France. However, this is my way and it is the best.

Serves 4–5

Hearts of 2 or 3 real lettuce, crisp leaves that are curled tightly together in a monochrome of green (not Chinese leaves, icebergs, etc.)
1 handful lightly cooked runner or French beans from your garden
8 ripe tomatoes, sliced
2 green tomatoes, sliced
½ teaspoon coarse ground sea salt
5 or 6 tablespoons olive oil
16 halves of hard boiled, ochre-yolked, free-range eggs
5 oz (150 g) glistening black olives (if packed in brine, drain, dry and marinate in olive oil)
9 oz (250 g) tuna fish, canned in olive oil
4 oz (110 g) anchovy fillets, canned in olive oil
1 can sardines in olive oil

Wash and thoroughly dry the lettuce and put into a large salad bowl. Add the beans, tomatoes, sea salt and olive oil. With your fingers, gently turn the salad until everything is coated with oil and salt.

Add all the other ingredients and, again with your fingers, carefully mix them together. As you lift your fingers from the bowl, bring the eggs and olives to the top as if you were fluffing up your hair after a shower.

If you do this with care, the result will be a naturally vibrant and colourful masterpiece, not the fussy concoction of a maniac who has substituted sterile style for freshness and taste.

Bitter Salad with Warm Scallops

The warm scallops liaise with the cold salad and dressing to make a delightful combination of flavours and textures.

Serves 4

2 oz (50 g) lamb's lettuce
1 oz (25 g) nasturtium leaves
1 heart of escarole (type of endive)
2 oz (50 g) red lettuce (radicchio)
2 cooked artichoke hearts, sliced
Olive oil, lemon juice, salt and pepper, for dressing the salad
2 oz (50 g) butter
14 oz (400 g) scallops, sliced into roundels
1 tablespoon chopped chervil

Toss the salad with the oil, lemon juice, salt and pepper in a salad bowl and then arrange attractively on individual plates. There should be plenty of lemon juice in the dressing.

Melt the butter in a frying pan and fry the scallops briskly for 2 or 3 minutes – they must not be overcooked. Place the scallops on the salad and garnish with chervil.

Herring and Potato Salad

This is a fantastic salad and takes no time to prepare, so long as you have bought herring fillets canned in oil.

Serves 4

1 lb (450 g) cold boiled potatoes, cut into ¼ in (6 mm) thick slices
10 oz (275 g) canned herrings (they sometimes come in plastic sachets, which are
    acceptable), cut into 1 in (2.5 cm) long pieces
1 large sweet onion, cut into very thin rings
2 tablespoons olive oil
1 tablespoon finely chopped parsley
Salt and pepper

Toss all the ingredients in a salad bowl, turn once or twice, chill and serve.

The Finest Prawn Cocktail in the World

Serves 4

2 oz (50 g) red lettuce (radicchio)
1 oz (25 g) fresh, young, small dandelion leaves
36 langoustines or freshwater crayfish or large prawns, freshly cooked, peeled and cold
    (saving 4 for garnish) – not frozen prawns
12 oz (350 g) cold, very fine French beans, cooked al dente (firm to the bite)
12 freshly cooked, cold asparagus spears
Pink sauce (see page 33)
4 fronds fennel for decoration

Arrange the lettuce and dandelion leaves in a small mound on large white plates. Divide the fish, beans, and asparagus elegantly among the four plates. Coat with the pink sauce and decorate with a whole langoustine and a frond of fennel.

Warm Seafood Salad

Serves 4

40 mussels, cooked *à la marinière* (see page 83) and removed from shells (retain the liquid)
Juice of 1 lemon
Salt and pepper
2½ fl oz (60 ml) double cream
8 scallops, simmered for 2 or 3 minutes in the strained mussel juice
8 oysters, simmered with the scallops for the last 1½ minutes
20 freshly cooked prawns or langoustines
7 oz (200 g) cooked, cold carrots, cut into thin julienne strips
7 oz (200 g) cooked, cold baby turnips, cut into thin julienne strips
14 oz (400 g) whole, fine green beans, cooked and cold
1 tablespoon chopped parsley and chervil, mixed
4 puff pastry shapes

Take just over ¼ pint (150 ml) of the liquid in which you have cooked the mussels. Strain and add the lemon juice, salt, pepper and cream and bring to the boil. Add the prawns, oysters, scallops and mussels and simmer for 2 or 3 minutes, until they have warmed up again.

Arrange the vegetables attractively on white plates. Add the warmed fish mixture and garnish with the chopped parsley and chervil and a puff pastry shape.

SHRIMPS AND SMALL PRAWNS

If you are lucky enough to catch or buy fresh prawns or shrimps (the frozen variety are more like crescent-shaped, salted blotting paper), then you should drop them into boiling seawater and turn off the heat at once. Leave for 10 minutes or so and allow to cool. Strain them and eat with your fingers, and have a friend butter some brown bread and pass you a wedge of lemon.

SKATE

As a kid a cheap treat was deep-fried skate wing from the fish and chip shop. You sucked the flesh off the many bones as you dawdled home, your eyes fixed to the pavement, scanning the gutter for a dropped sixpence or even a penny. Skate is still relatively cheap today and this simple recipe will please you if you are not a food snob.

Skate with Black Butter

Serves 4

4 skate wings, well washed and dried
Sea salt
Pepper
1 tablespoon chopped capers
1 tablespoon chopped parsley
3 oz (75 g) butter
3 tablespoons malt vinegar

Cover the skate wings with water, add some salt and 1 tablespoon of vinegar. Bring to the boil, skim and then simmer gently for 10 minutes or so. Drain the skate very carefully and peel off the skin from both sides.

While the fish is still hot, season with salt, black pepper, capers and parsley. Then quickly brown the butter in a small pan and pour over the fish.

Deglaze the pan with the remaining vinegar over a high heat. Reduce the vinegar to just a few drops and sprinkle on to the skate wings.

SOLE

Turbot is undoubtedly the queen of flat fish, but what of sole, plaice and lemon sole, I hear you cry. Why are there not 29 different ways of preparing a Dover sole in this book?

Well, the answer is simple. You can cook sole or fillets of sole in the same way as many of the recipes in this book for one thing, and for another Dover soles are so expensive that I think the best treatment a fresh fat one can receive is to skin it and grill it until it chars ever so slightly on the outside and the flesh is just pink on the bone. Then eat it with melted butter and lemon juice, poured extravagantly over.

Similarly, with plaice, lemon sole and the like – they are all best skinned, de-finned, grilled and served whole with a dish of minted new potatoes. Their flesh is too fragile for complicated poaching or baking, and so delicate that anything but the lightest sauce will ruin the flavour.

SPRATS

The poor little sprat is caught in huge quantities and callously turned into cat food or fertiliser, which is a great pity because these little dreams are really very tasty, nutritious and, hip hip hurray, cheap.

I remember one autumn night watching an open fishing boat, about 30 feet long, waddling through the narrow harbour mouth of West Bay like a heavily pregnant cat slinking down an alley, laden and rounded to the gunwales with sprats glinting in the moonlight. I took a bucketful home and feasted on charcoal grilled sprats moistened with lemon juice, washed down with pints of rough cider. And for breakfast there were pan-fried boned sprats on toast with lots of Worcestershire sauce. Yum, yum. And yet, you see, I am a bit of a hypocrite because I never buy them when they are available in the shops. Except sometimes a few smoked ones (known as brisling – a great delicacy in Holland, Germany and Scandinavia), to nibble while sipping the evening *apéritif*.

The following recipe is one that I came across in a little book called *Fish for Caterers* published by the Sea Fish Industry Authority. I have modified the quantities, since the original was for 50 portions. I must say that I have never seen sprats on any works canteen menu – perhaps they are reserved for the directors' dining-room

at
the top of
some tinted tower.

Stuffed Sprats

Serves 4

2 lb (scant kg) sprats, boned
Salt and pepper
9 oz (250 g) cream cheese with herbs (either make your own mix with chives or use, say, Boursin)
Flour for dredging
3 eggs, beaten
Fresh breadcrumbs for coating
Oil for deep frying

Season the sprats with salt and pepper and spread the insides with the cream cheese. Reform the shape of the fish. Dredge the fish in the flour, dip into the beaten egg and coat with breadcrumbs. Deep fry for about 4 minutes. Drain the sprats on kitchen paper and serve very hot. This dish makes a super cocktail snack – for the price of a pint!

SQUID

Squid is very popular in southern France, Spain and throughout the Mediterranean. Although great quantities are landed in the West of England, most of the catch goes for export. The demand in Britain is negligible, apart from Chinese and Italian restaurants, which is a pity because squid is a tasty and versatile food, and not expensive.

I suppose that on first sight squid can be a bit offputting; if cleaned correctly, however, it is very easy to use. Start to prepare the squid by

Mussels in White Wine;
Over: The Finest Prawn Cocktail in the World (*top*), Bitter Salad with Warm Scallops

cutting off the tentacles and head (1). You will be left with a sort of purse. Plunge your hand into this purse and pull out the intestines. (This slightly messy task may well have been performed by your friendly fishmonger.) Remove the 'plastic' bone, which is rather like a corset stay or collar stiffener (2). Now rinse well under water and peel off the thin outside film (3). Cut the purse lengthways and you are left with two sheets of white flesh. Trim the two pieces into rectangular shapes (4). Now you are ready to cook. Smaller squid are excellent for frying; the larger specimens are better used in recipes which involve a longer stewing process.

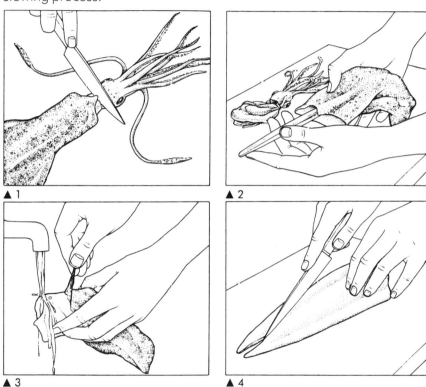

▲ 1

▲ 2

▲ 3

▲ 4

Stir-fried Squid
(From the China Garden, Plymouth)
Serves 4

1 ½ lb (700 g) prepared squid
Oil to cook
4 spring onions, chopped
1 carrot, cut into fine strips
2 cloves garlic, crushed
1 teaspoon finely chopped fresh ginger
½ glass rice wine or dry sherry
¼ pint (150 ml) chicken stock

With a very sharp knife, score the sheets of squid in a fine criss-cross pattern and cut into strips about 2 in (5 cm) long. When cooked, the strips will roll into delicate flowers.

Blanch the squid in fiercely boiling water for 2 minutes. Then strain and dry it. In another pan or wok, heat 2–3 tablespoons of bland cooking oil and stir-fry the squid for 2–3 minutes over maximum heat. Remove from the wok and keep hot.

Into the same oil, add all the other ingredients except for the chicken stock, and stir-fry for 2 minutes. Add the chicken stock and bubble furiously until the sauce thickens a little. Pour over the squid and eat with some plain boiled rice.

Deep Fried Squid

Start with 'sheets' of squid, as for the Stir-fried Squid recipe. Cut into longish strips, about ¼ in (6 mm) wide. Dredge in seasoned flour and deep fry in vegetable oil for 6–7 minutes. Mop off excess oil on kitchen paper and eat with lots of lemon juice.

You might like to roll them in flour first and then into beaten egg before frying. This will make a light puffy batter, but is easy to burn, so keep regulating the heat of the oil.

Stuffed Squid

You will need neat needlework to achieve best results with this, so when you order your 4 medium-sized and completely cleaned squid from your fishmonger, pop into the kitchen equipment shop and buy a needle and fine butcher's thread. Speak to the fishmonger nicely and ask for the tentacles to be chopped up and the squids prepared so as to give you white tubes into which you can force the stuffing. Stitch up the open end before cooking.

Serves 4

4 medium-sized squid, completely cleaned and prepared as above
2 fl oz (50 ml) olive oil
2 cloves garlic, crushed
14 oz (400 g) fresh ripe tomatoes, liquidised with 1 cup of water and strained to
    eliminate skin and pips
2 fl oz (50 ml) dry white wine
½ teaspoon rosemary spines

> **For the stuffing:**
> 3 tablespoons fresh breadcrumbs
> 2 tablespoons finely chopped parsley
> 6 tablespoons freshly grated Parmesan cheese
> Tentacles, finely chopped
> 2 cloves garlic, chopped
> 1 beaten egg
> Pinch cayenne pepper
> 2 tablespoons olive oil
> Juice of 1 lemon
> Pinch salt and freshly ground black pepper

Mix the stuffing ingredients together and stuff into the squids. Sew up the ends.

Heat the olive oil in a large pan and brown the garlic till the oil is flavoured. Discard the garlic and brown the stuffed squid on all sides. Add the tomatoes, white wine and rosemary and reduce the heat to low. Cover the dish and simmer gently for about 30 minutes, turning the squid carefully from time to time.

When cooked, slice the squid into fork-sized pieces with the stuffing intact, cover with the sauce and serve with some saffron-flavoured rice.

T

TROUT

With the profusion of signs saying 'Last Trout Farm Before Motorway', the trout, that wonderful fine-fleshed fish of my youth, has become something of a gastronomic joke. And trout with almonds is clichéd beyond belief. What was a few years ago a treat has today become the lazy restaurateur's token 'fish dish', and not only usually farmed but frozen as well. (Beware of restaurants that still have five ways of cooking trout and six of sole on menus that also offer 'pheasant in port' – in July – and duckling with marmalade, sorry I mean *à l'orange*.)

If you are to eat trout simply, say grilled or fried in butter, the farmed trout does need plenty of seasoning by way of salt and pepper and lemon juice, inside and out, and be sure to use a very hot grill so that the skin chars a bit.

For Truite Meunière, which is really the best way of cooking a trout, the essential thing, after frying your well-seasoned trout in butter, is to pop the fish on to a hot plate and throw away the butter that you have used to cook the fish. Add some fresh butter and bubble it up until it turns slightly brown at the edges and is foaming like a Cornish wave. Pour it at once over the fish and eat immediately.

Trout in Newspaper

During the course of some filming for television I once had cause to visit a trout farm in Devon. Although not exactly thrilled at the thought, things brightened up considerably when Caroline Boa cooked me a trout in newspaper. Well, what can I say? It was quite tasty, certainly novel, but the greatest advantage seemed to me to be that by careful selection of the newspapers used, one could insult or embarrass one's friends with puckish ease. Here is the recipe. Naturally, I use *The Times*:

1 trout per person, about 6 oz (175 g), cleaned and gutted
2 sheets newspaper per fish
Bouquet of fresh herbs per fish
Thin slice lemon per fish
Yoghurt sauce (see page 35)

Stuff the fish with herbs and a slice of lemon. Wrap an envelope of paper around each fish and run under the cold water tap until sodden.

Place in an oven at gas mark 4/350°F/180°C until the paper dries out completely – about 8 minutes. Using scissors, open the package and peel off the paper, which will lift off the skin of the trout. Decorate with yoghurt sauce.

TUNA

You are more likely to see 10 feet of tuna fish, a powerful dark blue torpedo-shaped thing, lying on a trestle table in the hot sun of a Mediterranean market place than upon the slab of British fishmongers; but this giant relation of the mackerel is available here and well worth buying. The flesh is dark and close-textured, like meat, and makes an ideal fish for grilling or barbecueing. The following method is one that I came across in the scented south of Spain:

Tuna Fish Grilled with Herbs

Serves 4

4 slices tuna, about 7 oz (200 g) each
Salt and pepper
Juice of 1 lemon
2 bay leaves, chopped
4 sage leaves, chopped
4 basil leaves, chopped
10 florets parsley, chopped
½ teaspoon chopped rosemary spines
½ teaspoon chopped thyme
3 tinned anchovy fillets, chopped
1 clove garlic, crushed
2 tablespoons olive oil

Wash and dry the slices of tuna. Put the fish on to a grilling tray and season with salt and pepper and lemon juice. Mix all the herbs, garlic, anchovies and oil and paint on to both sides of the fish and leave to marinate for 1 hour.

Grill the tuna under a fairly gentle grill, or barbecue, for 5 minutes each side.

TURBOT

The turbot is not only one of the most expensive flat fish, it is one of the most uneconomical because of wastage after being cleaned. It also has the reputation of being the finest of all flat fish, and I would not disagree.

I find the best way to cook turbot is by trimming the fins off, but leaving the head and skin on, and poaching gently in a court bouillon (see page 29). Lift the fish carefully from the pan, remove the skin and bones and serve with one of the following sauces: hollandaise (see page 32), Normande (see page 33), cardinal (see page 33) or *beurre blanc* (see page 31). And, in every case, some young samphire (sea-fennel), stir-fried in a bland oil for a minute or two, will make a divine side dish.

Turbot with Onions

Serves 4

3 lb (1 ½ kilos) turbot
20 small peeled fresh onions (no bigger than small walnuts), very finely chopped
4 tablespoons olive oil
Juice of 1 lemon
1 fl oz (25 ml) dry white wine
3 fresh tomatoes, skinned, depipped and puréed
1 carrot, peeled and finely sliced
Bouquet garni
Salt and pepper

Gut, clean, wash, trim and dry the turbot. Fry the chopped onions in the olive oil until golden. Moisten with lemon juice and wine. Add the tomato, carrots and bouquet garni and cook over a low heat for 20 minutes. Add salt and pepper to taste.

Place the turbot into a baking dish and cover with the sauce. If necessary, add a little water so that the fish is well moistened but not covered. Cover the dish and simmer gently for 20 minutes. Remove the fish to a serving dish and take off the skin.

Liquidise the sauce and strain over the fish. This dish, of course, can be served hot, but is also very good cold.

W

WHITEBAIT

This delightful little fish, often a tiny sprat, was once caught in large quantities in the Thames and other charming places such as Whitby Bay. Now it comes frozen in plastic bags, and is served as a starter in restaurants that usually have a Dickensian decor theme – which is where they should stay.

But if you do happen to find some fresh whitebait, there is no better way to cook them than by simply dipping them in milk, dredging in well-seasoned flour and deep frying. Serve with plenty of lemon pieces.

Z

ZARZUELA

I have only ever come across this fish in Spain, so I can't tell you the English name for it – I doubt if there is one. The first time I tasted it was in Tarifa, the small town which is even further south than Gibraltar and just across the water from Africa. There was a competition going on, featuring a game not unlike *boules*, but instead of being played with metal bowls in French style, it was being played with the empty husks of sea urchins – a sort of *boules marinières*. The locals told me that way back in Moorish days, the Moors used to play it with the skulls of the conquered Spaniards. I was persuaded to enter and managed to get through two rounds before it got too painful.

Anyway, they were cooking fish over an open fire, a delicious large fish with firm white flesh called zarzuela which is so rare that it is only found at the very beginning of April. Curiously, I found it the next time in the north of Spain, but at the end of September. The locals explained that the schools of zarzuela drift slowly up the Portuguese coast during the summer and land in the north of Spain at the end of the season before returning south for the winter. What was never explained to me was why the fish was now, not big and white, but small and red-skinned. I can only assume that we were eating the offspring of the ones I had seen in Tarifa.

They are best grilled over an open fire and washed down with good local wine. Don't forget – it is pronounced *tharthuela*.

Miles Kington kindly gave me this recipe – when he was a judge at the Bridport Scallop Festival (I was a judge, too, actually). I think it rounds the book off nicely.

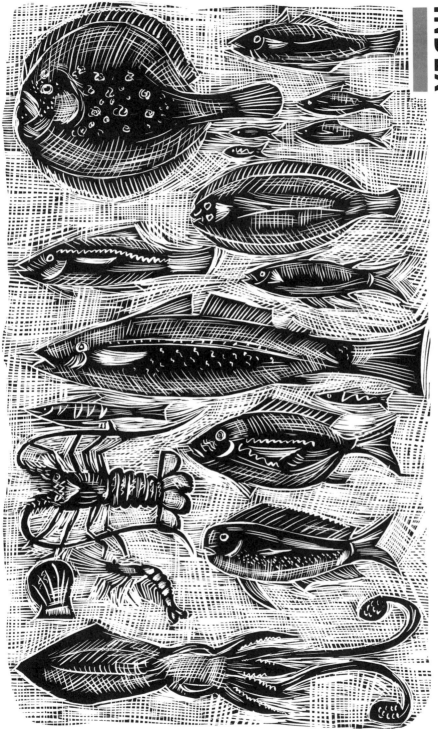